The Adam Connection

The Adam Connection

One Family Under God

Rob Faw

XULON PRESS

Xulon Press
2301 Lucien Way #415
Maitland, FL 32751
407.339.4217
www.xulonpress.com

Scripture quotations taken from the Holy Bible, New International Version
(NIV). Copyright © 1973, 1978, 1984 by International Bible Society. Used
by permission of Zondervan Publishing House. All rights reserved.

Scripture quotations taken from the New King James Version (NKJV).
Copyright © 1979, 1980, 1982 by Thomas Nelson, Inc. Used by permission. All rights reserved.

Scripture quotations taken from the King James Version (KJV)–*public domain.*

Scripture quotations taken from the Holy Bible, New Living Translation
(NLT). Copyright ©1996, 2004, 2007 by Tyndale House Foundation. Used
by permission of Tyndale House Publishers, Inc. Printed in the United
States of America.

ISBN-13: 9781545613467

Table of Contents

Acknowledgments

I must say that I'm eternally grateful for the power of the Holy Spirit that inspired me to research and write this story. It was on March 24, 2013, five days before Good Friday, that I was unexpectedly convicted to begin my search for wisdom and understanding about ancestry. A few months later, I remember speaking with my since-departed friend, Eddie Flom, author of *Thirty-Three: The Story of Hope*, about what I was experiencing. He wisely assessed that I had been called to tell this story, and my journey was about being perfected in Christ. That is what I understood and what I have been experiencing.

My wife Jill has steadfastly supported me along the way and my youngest son, Tommy, has been a rock of encouragement. My oldest son, Joey, helps me be better. In the late summer of 2013, my sister Beth and I visited our Aunt Ann in Waycross, Georgia. Our trip and that time with our father's sister-in-law was not only precious, but revealed ancestral stories that profoundly piqued my curiosity and accelerated my research and development of this non-fiction narrative.

Within a year, my wife and I visited my centenarian fourth cousin, Amanda Ray Bowers of Boone, North Carolina. Known by all as "Ray," this beloved woman is full of the light of Christ. Ray was my great-grandmother's first cousin. The Witherspoon's are somewhat legendary in the Appalachian region of the United States. Their ancestors were both colorful and impactful in their affect and contributions to the birth, division, and unification of our great nation. My seventh great grand-uncle, John Witherspoon, was a signer of the Declaration of Independence.

I humbly acknowledge my eleventh great-grandfather, John Knox, widely known and respected as one of the leaders of the Protestant Reformation, and considered the founder of the Presbyterian Church in Scotland. I hope and pray that this story blesses his memory and leadership in expanding Christianity throughout Europe and around the world.

I appreciate the encouragement, guidance, and collaboration with my friends and colleagues at the Arthur J. Custance Centre for Science and Christianity, especially Dr. Gary Chiang and Evelyn White. Many other family members, friends, and colleagues have influenced me and my writing including my since-departed sister Kathy, sisters Peggy, Colleen, and my second cousin, Shirley Daniel. I am so appreciative of my executive coach, Dwight Bain along with Debi Alberdi, Kirk Berendes, Jerome Ciliento, Jason Clement, Doug DeBoer, Stephen DeFrancesco, John Galligan, Charlie Giannetto, Jim and Peggy Fulford, Reverend Joan Hill, David Hoffman, Barry and Luronda Joye, Erin Lindsey, Brian Lawandus, John and Nicole Matuska, Ana Mira, Dr. Daniel Mullett, Dr. Glen Pettersen, Matt Ramker, Keith Sadlowski, Sal Ventimiglia, Allen Wetherilt, Mary Wutschel, Kate Rogers, and my small-group friends and believers at Safety Harbor Community Church.

I'm especially grateful, on so many levels, for my compadre David; and dear friend, brother in Christ, and colleague, Jay Hill. My Starbucks family have endured and supported my endless reading, thinking, and writing in their presence. I appreciate their friendship, especially, Richard Salladin, Sally McKinney, Peggy Dalton, Dan Kistel, Lowell, and the entire Safety Harbor Starbucks team led by Michelle Cherny.

My twenty-eighth cousin, and confidant, Ed Robie, has been so helpful in shaping my thoughts, words, and writing. We are joined by our love of Christ, shared values, and a bloodline that goes back to eleventh century Scotland.

My dearest friend and brother, Michael Clemons, has been a blessing in my life. I appreciate his leadership, love of the Lord, commitment to community, and to empowering youth through education.

I would like to particularly recognize Virginia Brown, Jeff Ford, and Katie Matuska for their time, expertise, and feedback to help me develop and edit the manuscript. They were so helpful in shaping my storytelling.

Doug Webber has been a great friend and branding expert who helped me develop the name for this story. Doug's wife Lorena is a special person who selflessly encourages others, including me, in her circle of influence at work, home, and the community.

Rich Hayes and his team at Digital Lightbridge, particularly Renee Burgdorf and Katelyn Hlavaty, have been wonderfully supportive in all things related to strategic marketing. I respect Rich and his team so much and appreciate their mission to share the love of Jesus while creating marketing solutions with excellence.

Finally, my publishing, print, editorial, and marketing team at Xulon Press and Salem Author Services are simply the best, especially the guidance and support I have received from Bethany Emerson, Jason Fletcher, Glorimar Guzman, Jennifer Kasper, Michelle Johnston, Don Newman, Toni Riggs, and Dr. Larry Keefauver.

For those that I've recognized, and others that I have overlooked, thank you all for your love and support of me in developing this story that was 6,000 years in the making.

Preface

Several years ago, I became unexpectedly curious about my own family ancestry. My wife reminded me that fifteen years earlier, my oldest sister had researched and written a family history paper, and her recordings were in our storage files. I remember previously glancing through the paper, but never really took the time to read it. To my surprise, I was quite intrigued to discover more about my family origins. I promptly crawled through our files and discovered a typewritten paper with some handwritten notes that traced our ancestry back fifteen generations to sixteenth century Europe. The depth and breadth of my sister's research quite frankly astonished me. I found myself in a whole new world of child-like bewilderment. I experienced powerful feelings related to my connection with other family members and generations in the past.

Tracing my ancestry was exciting. However, the more deeply I learned about our family history, the more I found myself connecting with past generations. The more stories I uncovered about my ancestors, the more appreciation I had for their sacrifices, perseverance, and life experiences. I also experienced wide-eyed humility after learning about past family member misbehaviors, wrongdoings, and transgressions including a nineteenth century tragedy that played out in the U.S. national media.

I came across astounding stories that included seventeenth century persecutions against my ancestors from religious and ethnic intolerance. My family members have defended liberty since the eighteenth century and in the nineteenth century, fervently supported civil rebellion in the bloodiest war in U.S. history. Surprisingly, some of the most prominent men in U.S. history were family members who led the fight against tyranny, provided leadership for world-class education institutions, and helped architect the United States Constitution.

I uncovered stories about bloodline relatives born out of wedlock and those who offended human dignity. Amazingly, I learned about those who led a religious and cultural movement that shaped the history of the world. I was soberly reminded of the personal challenges affecting generations of mothers, fathers, children, and families. They were all living, loving, surviving, and thriving in a turbulent and changing world.

By discovering my family roots, I became overwhelmed with a deep appreciation for the human family, all of whom I'm certain, have amazing stories of their own. What developed in my heart was a profound gratitude for the long-odds of my sheer existence.

What humbled me most about the process were the stories about previous generations. My curiosity had evolved to a near-fanatical pursuit of each new tidbit of information. As I submerged myself in libraries, archives, books, the Internet, and other repositories of information, I became passionately more interested in history, and my connection with previous generations. I continued to research all available sources in the hope that every day would provide a brand-new lead to be explored or the discovery of one new connection.

Along the way, I experienced one of those connections that can hardly be explained. Several years before I started my research, I began working with a businessman. From the first day we met, I just felt a connection. We were different in many ways, but we seemed to share common values. Our backgrounds and experiences were completely different. Yet, we harmonized as trusted colleagues from the very first day. I could not explain it. I did not understand it, but it was there. He and I just connected. In a very short period, we were becoming best friends. After several shared business experiences and traveling with each other throughout North America, somewhat by happenstance we learned that we had a common great-grandfather dating back to the fourteenth century. My new best friend and business associate was a distant cousin!

After I discovered my new cousin, I reconnected with a ninety-year-old aunt and met a one-hundred-year-old cousin, both of whom shared stories that could only be told by elders from one generation to the next. Their stories vividly brought to life our ancestors' involvement in the battles and blessings of bygone eras that extended back through World War II, World War I, The Civil War, The Revolutionary War, and the Protestant Reformation, which originated in Europe five-hundred years earlier.

These insights and unexpected revelations hastened my search for wisdom and understanding of past generations, with the idea of developing a connection theory that might apply to all humankind. In the beginning of this intentional search, I first turned to the sacred writings of Christianity in the Bible, because I believed God would inform me about my theory of the humankind connection.

> *Remember the days of old, consider the years of all generations. Ask your father, and he will inform you, your elders, and they will tell you.*
>
> (Deuteronomy 32:7 NIV)

God's appointed servant, Moses, the Egyptian Prince and biblical prophet in Judaism, Christianity, and Islam, expressed those prophetic words in fifteenth century BC as he led the Israelites to a place on earth where his nation could be a free people under the rule of God. I completely and without qualification, connected with this prophecy concerning the wisdom of elders and consideration of the years of all generations.

My journey for wisdom and understanding led to what became an intense generational investigation of ancient, medieval, and modern history. The result of my pursuit is the telling of this 6,000-year old, 144-generational story that connects Adam, the first man in the Bible, to Queen Elizabeth II.

I'm intrigued by the science of complexity and the notion that everything in the world may very well be interconnected. Complexity can be found in structures such as weather patterns, organizations, or ecosystems. The premise of complexity is that systems sometimes generate energy in unpredictable directions resulting in chaos. The Chaos Theory, a branch of mathematics that studies dynamic systems, can model complex, nonlinear things that are effectively impossible to predict or control.

MIT professor, Edward Lorenz, the author of The Chaos Theory and Butterfly Effect, observed the flap of a butterfly's wings in Brazil can set off a tornado in Texas. Essentially, the mathematical modeling in The Chaos Theory can predict there is a relationship between every molecule of air on the planet.

I believe this scientific theory can be extended to a perspective that the complex, chaotic dynamics of our global society are also interconnected. With a deeper understanding of an interconnected global society, we can hope to avoid actions which may end up being detrimental to the long-term well-being of humankind.

Are We All Connected?

If there is a relationship between everything,
how is it that every person in the world is related?

What is the nature of our relationship with each other?

How are we connected?

Is our connection with each other just as an evolved species from primates,
or is it something else?

What if our connection with each other is much more profound
than an evolved species?

What if we are divinely connected as humankind ancestors?

What if this human connection between everyone can be demonstrated
with considered and compelling evidence?

Such an idea would indeed be infinitely more interesting, satisfying, and eternally meaningful. At the same time, such an idea can only be personally confirmed by what we each believe to be true.

As a Science and Christianity researcher, I seek to discern information to gain knowledge with understanding. My graduate studies in global leadership have ingrained in me to continually consider cross-cultural worldviews, ideas, and geopolitical similarities and differences between people and nations. I am mindful to consider both secular and religious scholarship, and have been trained to follow the evidence with humility.

With all that in mind, the process of studying and researching six thousand years of history has been invigorating, enlightening, and mostly humbling. I believe the evidence for this narrative, *The Adam Connection*, provides insights that can connect every one of us to each other.

This historical account is not necessarily about theology, doctrine, or dogma of any religion. However, I believe that to consider the continuity and connectedness of humankind after the creation of Adam and Eve, it is essential to consider the existence of God. As such, this narrative is about the people, history, and cultures that over time connect Adam, created in the image of God, and the Queen of England. While this connection is not exclusively about monarchy or famous people, the story brings ancient and medieval history to life within the context of those times. Research by historians, philosophers, scientists, and academic and biblical scholars provide clarity, contradictions, and ultimately an understanding of enduring possibilities.

More than ever, cultural, and religious differences have created systemic misunderstandings and disconnections between people within our global society. Moreover, for much of the world, contradictions between science and religion have been undermining the consideration, let alone belief, in God's existence. For example, different beliefs regarding human origins can detract from exploring the existence of God and developing an understanding of an ancestral relationship between all humankind and God. While science can provide understanding of the natural world, it is religion that provides understanding of God and the supernatural. I believe it is religion that has provided us with a historical, reliable account of the existence of God and a man named Adam, who was the first person created by God.

The story of God and Adam was first told in the first book (Genesis) of the Old Testament in the Christian Bible. In Judaic tradition, Genesis is also the first book of The Torah or the Pentateuch. Genesis recounts the events from God's creation of the world to the dwelling of the Israelites in Egypt. Yet, the story of humankind that was begun in Genesis, continues to this day.

The etymology (origin of words) of the word Genesis, is from the seventeenth century Old English word, *Genesis* which was derived from the Greek word, *genesis* meaning "origin, creation, generation." The Greek origin of Genesis is *gignesthai* which means "to be born" and *genos* meaning "race, birth, descent." The Hebrew word *bereshith*, literally means "in the beginning" which was the first word of the text, taken as its title in the Bible and the Torah.

I've chosen to focus on the Adam to Queen Elizabeth lineage, because it is their ancestry which has the most complete information that could be discerned from ancient and medieval documents. Most scholars agree that Adam would have been born in the Middle East and his descendants would ultimately flourish from three brothers who populated the regions of Asia, Middle East, and Africa, Europe, and the rest of the world.

It is the ancient Middle East and medieval European scholarship that provide the richest sources of information for this story. As such, these ancient and medieval resources provide the most reasonable and justifiable basis for documenting this one family under God that originated in the Middle East, migrated eastward across North Africa, and then northward from Spain to Ireland, Scotland, and the United Kingdom.

The Adam Connection ties Adam and Queen Elizabeth II together over a period of 6,000 years and 144 generations. Their connection by origin, race, generations, and descent is both incredible and imaginable. We can now boldly connect two of the most famous people in the history of the world.

The unexpected evidence of their connection can, therefore, reasonably connect Adam to every man, woman, and child who has ever lived. I believe this one family under God, provides evidence for a humankind connection theory that is not only possible, but probable.

We are all connected!

Perhaps current and future generations can now consider a new way of thinking about our connection with each other and the existence of God. I'm honored to tell this continuing story of humankind from the very beginning.

Introduction

The Humankind Connection Theory

By way of introduction, I must say that I believe *The Adam Connection* is a big and hopeful idea filled with intrigue, contradictions, and unity. As a Christian, my primary interest is to be "in" this world, but not be "of" this world. For me, being "in" this world is to live and love others as God loves us while not being "of" this world and following worldly values, beliefs, and behaviors. Being in this world is about my relationship with God and abiding in Him to guide my values, beliefs, and behaviors. I believe in God, and have no concerns or reservations about who He is and my relationship with Him. As such, my worldview is framed from a believing perspective.

However, God has given me the gift of a love for learning. I'm deeply and passionately curious. I love the complexity of this big idea of the humankind connection theory. Yet, this same complexity has been like a puzzle perfectly falling into place for our collective consideration. Once I embraced the journey and opened my heart and mind to consider the evidence wherever it might lead, I also journeyed to a place of peace and joy. During this journey as my relationship with God inevitably strengthened, my relationship with others in the world became stronger than ever.

I have grown to see everyone in the world, literally, as my ancestral family.

The idea of connecting two of the most famous people in the world over 6,000 years could have been overwhelming, yet it has not really been a heavy lift. Yes, the research has been deeply time consuming. Discerning the many natural and supernatural contradictions since ancient times has been a wonderful challenge. Still, the connection between God, Adam, and Queen Elizabeth II found its path.

I have had to consider the very existence of God and what influence history and science can have on a person's belief in God. I have tried to highlight some of the challenges to a person's belief since the Age of Enlightenment, and the role of rational and reasonable thinking. I'm mindful that *The Adam Connection* is a theory of sorts and that the reader will ultimately determine what he or she believes. How wonderful it is that I do not have to convince anyone of anything. I merely have to reveal what I have learned about this remarkable connection and let everyone decide for themselves.

I'm also mindful that one must diligently research ancient and medieval history to extract the many conflicting accounts of the past; then hopefully weave it all together into a coherent narrative that may provide some further understanding as to who we are and where we came from. It is not my intention to offend anyone with this narrative. However, I do want to encourage and challenge everyone to stir their hearts, minds, and souls and reflect on what this big idea may personally mean to you.

C.S. Lewis, the British novelist, academic, and Christian apologist, once remarked that belief in God is not something that one can moderately be interested in.

If God does not exist, then there is no reason to be interested in God at all. If God does not exist, then life is ultimately meaningless and destined to end in death, so it would not matter how we lived our lives. If God does not exist, then life is ultimately lived without hope of being delivered from evil, disease, aging, and ultimately death after our limited existence.

On the other hand, if God does exist, then it is in our eternal best interest to know how we relate to Him. We would want to know Him in a very personal way, so we can live our lives with meaning and hope. We would want to love and enjoy Him.

Given a choice, it is perfectly rational to believe in God. On the other hand, it is irrational to believe that God does not exist; preferring death, futility, and despair over hope, meaning, and joy.[1]

Lord John Dalberg-Acton, the nineteenth century Victorian political thinker and historian, observed that the study of history ought to be the strongest influence in the formation of character. He noted that knowledge of history means choice of ancestors.[2] Lord Acton also commented that man must live both in the future and the past. He who does not live in the past does not live in the future. Each age is an essential of the world's history, and has influence and lessons for the future.[3]

This sense and understanding of history certainly matters in providing context for a belief in God's existence. The Age of Enlightenment,

---

[1] William Lane Craig, Does God Exist? (Reasonable Faith, 2016).

[2] John Dalberg-Acton, Essays in Religion, Selected Writings of Lord Acton (Indianapolis, Liberty Fund, 1988), 620.

[3] Ibid., 621.

sometimes called the Age of Reason, refers to the time of a guiding intellectual movement in Europe that began in 1620 with the publication of Francis Bacon's *Novum Organum Scientiarum* (New Instrument of Science), a book about reason. Bacon, and the Enlightenment thinkers who followed, argued that reason could free humankind from religious authoritarianism that brought death and suffering to millions in religious wars.

About four hundred years since the Age of Enlightenment began, there has been an exciting growth and development of the physical and life sciences. Regrettably, the Enlightenment also resulted in a decline in religious beliefs to only those essentials that could be rationally defended. These rational essentials include basic moral principles to do good, avoid evil, and practice fairness as well as a few universally held beliefs in a creator and how the spiritual conflicts with the soul.

While progress in science has resulted in greater understanding of the world, that same progress has created contradictions with certain philosophical and theological considerations in modern, medieval, and ancient history.

Pope John Paul II observed that while modern rationalism cannot be blamed for the move away from Christianity, such an estrangement became possible. The rationalism of Enlightenment put God to one side. Since the existence of God was not always helpful to science, it was also necessary to act as if God did not exist or if He did, He was disinterested in the world. The rationalism of Enlightenment could not accept God outside of the world, primarily because it was an unverifiable hypothesis. It was essential that God be excluded from the world.[4]

The exclusion of God from the world is incompatible with the origins and development of Western philosophy, which began in the fourth

---

[4] John Paul II, Go in Peace, A Gift of Enduring Love (Chicago, Loyola Press, 2003), 53.

century BC, with such classical Greek philosophers as Socrates and his students, Plato and Aristotle. While science has made and continues to make many contributions towards a better understanding of the world, science cannot justify certain beliefs about biblical history and the existence of God.

Alvin Plantinga is an American analytic philosopher widely known for his work in the philosophy of religion, epistemology, metaphysics, and Christian apologetics. He says that it is within one's intellectual rights to believe in God, if one has not violated any intellectual responsibilities in the formation and sustenance of that belief. Said another way, it is "rational" and "reasonable" to believe in God. There is adequate justification to make a belief in God reasonable.[5]

This same justification can be applied to the assessment of biblical and historical works produced by scholars prior to the Enlightenment. It is rational and reasonable to do so. It is irrational to look back over the history of time from solely a lens of modern day beliefs formed since the Age of Enlightenment.

Viktor Frankl, the Austrian neurologist, psychiatrist, and Holocaust survivor, said that love is the only way to grasp the innermost core of a human being, and that no one can become fully aware of another person, unless he loves him. By his love, the loving person enables the beloved person to actualize the potential within him.[6]

> *He who does not love does not know God, for God is love.*
> (1 John 4:8 NKJV)

---

[5] Greg, Koukl, *Is It Rational to Believe in God?* (Stand to Reason, 2013).

[6] Viktor Frankl, *Man's Search For Meaning, An Introduction to Logotherapy* (New York, Simon and Schuster, 1984), 116.

While this historical narrative is not primarily about religion, it is undeniable that religion has profoundly influenced the annals of history. In the latter part of the twentieth century, conventional wisdom held that religion was on the decline and that the study of religion was of little importance in understanding the world. However, in the early part of the twenty-first century, religion has been assuming increased prominence in academic fields including history, sociology, and international relations. One of the first sociologists to recant the demise or even disappearance of religion, has been Peter Burger, founder of the Institute of Culture, Religion, and World Affairs.

Religious surveys are included in approximately half of the world's national censuses. The 2010 research study, *World's Religions in Figures*, reports that 55.5 percent of the world's population believe in God. Those God-believing religions include Judaism, Christianity, and Islam. Not only does much of the world believe in God, world religions are expected to grow over the next generation.

For example, Christianity comprises 32.8 percent of the world's population. Christianity is not declining, in fact it is projected to grow to 35.8 percent of the world's population by 2050—a steady 9 percent growth during the next generation.[7]

Most people in the world believe that God does exist because belief in Him is reasonable and rational. Science and the Age of Enlightenment are not the final authorities with respect to the existence of God and belief in Him.

---

[7] Todd Johnson, The World's Religions in Figures, (Chichester, John Wiley & Sons, 2013), xxi.

God's Creation of Adam

The Adam Connection begins with the biblical story of God's creation of Adam in the Garden of Eden. The exact location of Adam's creation is unknown, but thought by biblical scholars to be generally somewhere in the Middle East, perhaps in the Tigris-Euphrates River Valley. Modern-day geology and topography of the Middle East does not readily reveal the exact location, however, guidance by the Bible, and forensic study of the region's geology, suggests that present-day Israel was the central location of the Garden of Eden.[8]

William F. Albright, the twentieth century American archaeologist and biblical scholar has praised the Bible as being the single most accurate source document from history. Repeatedly, the Bible has been found to be accurate in its places, dates, and records of events. Few critics dare to question the geographical or ethnological reliability of the Bible.[9]

So, with God's creation of Adam, his wife Eve, and their descendants over the course of history, we can discern the course of a 6,000-year connection between the first man created by God and Queen Elizabeth II of England.

In biblical times, women were not traditionally listed in Old Testament genealogies, however, both women and men played a vital role in recorded history. In the first century AD, the Gospel writers represented women during the explanation of Jesus' lineage including that of his mother, Mary, who is included in the list of generations preceding her son.

The Adam Connection drama highlights everyday, transcendent women who shaped and influenced the history of the world. While

---

[8] The Lost Rivers of the Garden of Eden (KJV Bible).

[9] Biblical Data Are Historically Testable (Institute for Creation Research, 2016).

the narrative begins in the Middle East, subsequent generations traversed through modern day Ukraine, Egypt, Israel, North Africa, Spain, Ireland, Scotland, and England. The 144 generations in this adventure include eighty-nine kings and queens, and some of the most influential people in history who were not only heads of their families, but leaders of cities, regions, countries, cultures, and civilizations.

The generations in this dramatic adventure experienced the emergence, rise, interactions, achievements, and falls of civilizations, beginning with ancient Sumer in the historical southern region of Mesopotamia. The account of civilizations has been explored at length by distinguished historians, sociologists, and anthropologists.

Of the twelve major historical civilizations, seven no longer exist. The remaining five are Chinese, Japanese, Indian, Islamic, and Western. In the contemporary world, we can add Orthodox Latin American and possibly African civilizations.

It should be noted that key objective elements which define civilizations include blood, language, a way of life, and religion. Beginning with the Greeks, religion has been emphasized, and usually considered the most important foundation.[10]

The Adam Connection is a narrative that is told in twelve periods or "Ages" of history that were led by important men and women. This historical account reveals the passing of generations, as well as interesting personal accounts, and important cultural influences in their lives.

This journey begins with the premise that it is rational and reasonable to believe in God. Further, there is reason to believe that the Bible and other ancient historical records are reliable and if in doubt,

---

[10] Samuel Huntington, The Clash of Civilizations and the Remaking of World Order (New York, Simon & Schuster, 1996), 40-45.

plausible. Despite the sins of humankind throughout recorded history, Christianity is projected to continue its growth over the next decades.

The historical dates in *The Adam Connection* require some type of context. This literary non-fiction is founded on the premise of God. Since much of the reference material originated from ancient biblical and medieval sources, dates will be referenced using the traditional terms *anno Domini* (AD) and *before Christ* (BC). The term anno Domini is Medieval Latin, which means "in the year of the Lord." Science writer Robert Coolman said that the Scythian monk Dionysius Exiguus (Dionysius the Humble) first introduced the AD system in AD 525, counting the years since the birth of Christ.[11]

The Adam Connection is not only an account of enduring love that began with the creation of Adam, but it also recounts a long history of disgraceful battles. From the first recorded death in Adam's family when Cain murdered Abel to the over sixty-million people killed in World War II, humankind has had countless battles as a result of hatred, idolatry, jealousy, envy, rage, greed, malice, evil desires, and selfish ambition.

Since the first love between a man and a woman and the more than one hundred billion lives that followed, the fruits of the spirit have blessed humankind. The immeasurable blessings over these 6,000 years have been the result of connections from love, joy, peace, patience, kindness, goodness, faithfulness, gentleness, and self-control.

Before we delve into this 6,000-year generational story, let's consider a few more questions that we will endeavor to answer as we take this journey through history.

What is the influence of philosophy considering various theories of knowledge, experience, existence, and reason?

---

[11] Robert Coolman, Keeping Time: The Origin of B.C. & A.D. (Live Science).

What are the contradictions of science and religion that have had an influence on beliefs about world history?
What are the key records of history, and are they valid, especially in the modern-day Age of Enlightenment?
Does the uniqueness of man have any meaning in Creation?
Finally, what is the creation of God?

Based on radiometric dating techniques, most archaeologists and historians believe recorded human history began around the thirtieth century BC. This view of recorded history began with the Sumerian Cuneiform script. This script is one of the earliest systems of writing, distinguished by its marks on clay tablets, made by a blunt reed used as a stylus. In this view, the world's first culture would have begun in Mesopotamia which today would include most of Iraq, Kuwait, eastern parts of Syria, and southeastern Turkey.

Alternatively, based on ancient Egyptian, Sumerian, Aramaic, Hebrew, and Greek texts, many biblical scholars and historians believe that civilized human history began around the fortieth century BC. The world's recorded history would, therefore, have begun with the fifteenth century BC writings by Moses, the author/compiler of the first five books of the Old Testament in the Bible. As previously noted, the forensic study of regional geology, along with guidance from the Bible, suggests that civilization began in the Garden of Eden in present day Israel.

In both worldviews, complex civilizations emerged throughout the Middle East, and then expanded to India, western Asia, China, Europe, and Central and South America.

Recorded history is, therefore, considered to cover a span of roughly five to six thousand years depending on your worldview. It should be noted that the earliest dates of recorded history are approximate and dependent on the interpretative theories of various scientists and scholars.

In some cultures, legends and oral traditions are considered historical in nature, but unauthenticated in writing. While legends may represent traditional stories about history, perhaps even substantiated by archaeological and DNA findings, these stories can become marginalized over time through the lens of modern-day historians or scientists. The historians and scientists often choose to undermine the integrity of legendary stories, because these stories may be unverifiable using traditional, scientific means of verification.

So, what is the most reasonable and reliable evidence to develop a narrative that could connect all of humankind?

While acknowledging the different constructs by which science and religion have determined the origin of recorded human history, there is substantial evidence that God does in fact exist. Considerable evidence affirms that human beings have superior brains which can write, learn, and reflect on the developments of science, religion, and history. Therefore, it would be reasonable to interpret recorded ancient and medieval history, based on a philosophy of history known as epistemology, which is an investigation of what distinguishes justified belief from opinion.

The epistemology for *The Adam Connection* is based on interpreting medieval and ancient history through a lens of rational, reasonable, and justified belief that considers written evidence, and discerns the applications of both science and religion. Thus, the narrative for *The Adam Connection* is based on written ancient and medieval records primarily gleaned from *The Irish Chronicles, Annals of the World,* and the *Holy Bible.*

The Holy Bible

The first eleven chapters of Genesis give a brief outline of history from the creation of the universe, Adam and Eve, and subsequent migrations of humankind from the Middle East to all corners of the world.

Many scholars, including John O'Hart, the nineteenth century genealogist and author of *Irish Pedigrees (1892)*, believe that for ancient Semitic (Hebrew, Arabic, Aramaic) writers the idea of a genealogy was not so much a succession of persons, but rather of periods of time.

Ancient records of history are filled with connections of prominent events and people. O'Hart wrote that great leaps of time often occurred from the record of some historic person to a successor. Other scholars and researchers believe that many of the events, dates, and people in the Bible are "representative" and should not be considered literal.

No other ancient book is more studied, questioned, or maligned than the Bible.

The books of the Bible are a collection of sacred texts in Judaism and Christianity. By the time of the Protestant Reformation in 1517, Christians had been using seventy-three books in their Bibles (forty-six in the Old Testament, twenty-seven in the New Testament). They were considered divinely inspired text for more than 1100 years. This practice changed in the sixteenth century following the Reformation, when nine deuterocanonical books were dropped from the Christian Old Testament, resulting in a Protestant Bible that contains thirty-nine books in the Old Testament and twenty-seven in the New Testament.

While there has been extensive scholarly study and considered theology with respect to God and the number of books in the Bible, the established Bible varies depending on traditions or groups. The Christian Old Testament overlaps with the Hebrew Bible and the Greek Septuagint. The Hebrew Bible is known in Judaism as the Tanakh.

Roman Catholics, Anglicans, and Eastern Orthodox Christians stress the harmony and importance of biblical text along with sacred tradition. Protestant churches focus on the idea of *sola scriptura*, translated from Latin as "scripture alone." The concept of *sola scriptura* arose during the Reformation and many Christian denominations today support the use of the Bible as the only source of Christian teaching.

The Dead Sea Scrolls, discovered by a monastic religious community in 1949 at Qumran, Israel, confirmed the reliability of accepted Old Testament text. These ancient texts, found hidden in cliff-top caves, included one complete Old Testament book (Isaiah) and thousands of fragments, representing every Old Testament book except Esther. They were copied and studied by the Essenes, a member of an ancient Jewish sect in Palestine. The Dead Sea Scrolls date from the third century BC to the first century and provide the earliest window found so far into the texts of the Old Testament.

The New Testament is a collection of writings by early Christians, believed to be mostly Jewish disciples of Christ. These writings were by Greeks in the first century from about AD 48 to 95. More than 5,300 Greek manuscripts of the New Testaments were written. These early Christian Greek writings consist of narratives, letters, and apocalyptic writings. Altogether, there are 24,633 Syriac, Latin, Coptic, and Aramaic texts of the ancient New Testament that confirm the integrity and modern-day translations of scripture.

The oldest complete copy of the New Testament was discovered at St. Catherine's Monastery (located near Mount Sinai) in 1844 by New Testament scholar Konstantin von Tischendorf. "The manuscript, dated around AD 360 to 375, is one of the two oldest vellum (treated animal hide) manuscripts of the Greek New Testament." His discovery has proven vital to scholars and translators in verifying New Testament accuracy and reproduction across the ages.[12]

---

[12] Christian Classic Ethereal Library, Lobegott Friedrich Konstantin Von Tischendorf.

**Growing evidence suggests that the Bible manuscripts
are undeniably accurate.**

For example, the Jewish scribes who copied by hand the manuscripts
of the Old Testament were called Masoretic, derived from the Hebrew
word for "wall" or "fence." They exercised extreme care in counting the
letters of the Bible and created a "fence around the Law" to defend the
accuracy of the biblical text.

Out of the 78,064 Hebrew letters that make up the book of
Genesis, there were only nine letters that varied from 304,805 letters
in the Yemenite Torah manuscript translated some 1,000 years after the
Masoretic translation. This represented an accuracy of 99.99705 percent
with none of those nine variant letters changing the meaning of a significant word in the Torah.[13]

Genesis

As previously noted, the first book of the Bible is Genesis, which in
Greek is defined as "origin." Depending on its context, genesis can mean
"birth," "genealogy," or "history of origin." Genesis speaks of beginnings,
of heaven and earth, of light and darkness, of seas and skies, of land and
vegetation, of sun, moon, and stars, of sea, of land, animals, and of human
beings made in God's image. The first eleven chapters of Genesis intro-
duce the Creator God and the beginnings of life, sin, judgement, family,
worship, and salvation.

On the first day, God created light, then the sky and oceans on the
second day, and then dry land on the third day. On the fourth day, God

---

[13] Grant R. Jeffrey, The Signature of God,(WaterBrook Press, Colorado Springs, 2010),
18-19.

created the sun, moon, and stars. On the fifth day, God created the birds and fish. On the sixth day, God said, "Let the earth produce every sort of animal, each producing offspring of the same kind–livestock, small animals that scurry along the ground, and wild animals." God saw that it was good.

> *Then God said, "Let us make human beings in our image, to be like us. They will reign over the fish in the sea, the birds in the sky, the livestock, all the wild animals of the earth, and the small animals that scurry along the ground." So, God created human beings in his own image. In the image of God he created them; male and female he created them. Then God blessed them and said, "Be fruitful and multiply. Fill the earth and govern it. Reign over the fish in the sea, the birds in the sky and all the animals that scurry along the ground." (Genesis 1:24-28 NLT)*

With an estimated total sale of over 5 billion copies, the Bible is considered the best-selling book of all time.

As of September 2016, Wycliffe Global Alliance estimates the full Bible has been translated into over 554 languages and 2,932 languages have had at least some portion of the Bible translated. The Bible has been a major influence on literature and history, especially in Western civilization since the invention of the Gutenberg printing press and the first mass-printed Gutenberg Bible.

Although the Bible continues to be relentlessly attacked by secular society, it still stands as the most authoritative and accurate book ever written. Archeological discoveries during the past century support the accuracy of the Bible. This includes revealed ancient references to forty-one kings of Israel and the surrounding nations that were identified in the Old Testament.

Jewish archaeologist, Dr. Nelson Glueck, stated categorically in his book, *Rivers in the Desert*, that no archaeological discovery has ever controverted a biblical reference. The Bible has been documented for accuracy to a far greater extent than secular documents from the same eras.[14]

K.A. Kitchen, the Honorary Research Fellow at the School of Archaeology, Classics, and Oriental Studies at the University of Liverpool, diligently researched and wrote a spirited defense of the Old Testament in his book, *On the Reliability of the Old Testament (2003)*. While leaning heavily on secular history, archaeological findings, and scientific methods, Professor Kitchen eschewed theology and biblical literalism to impressively refute those who could or would not consider the Holy Bible as a validated record of history.

Josh McDowell, the Christian apologist, evangelist, and author or co-author of some 115 books, including *Evidence That Demands a Verdict (1999)*, says, "Now here's the picture: 1,600 years, 60 generations, 40-plus authors, different walks of life, different places, different times, different moods, different continents, three languages, writing on hundreds of controversial subjects and yet when they are brought together, there is absolute harmony from beginning to end...There is no other book in history to even compare to the uniqueness of this continuity."[15]

The remarkable structure of the Bible seamlessly weaves together a story so intricate and balanced that chance, collusion, and unreliability are incomprehensible. The theme of the Bible is God's great work in the Creation and redemption of all things. When compared to other ancient

---

[14] Tim Chaffey, 3 Evidences That Confirm the Bible is Not Made Up, 2017.

[15] Ray Comfort, Scientific Facts in the Bible, (Bridge-Logos, Alachua, FL 32615), 73.

documents, the Bible stands far above other written documents from that era in terms of historical accuracy and archaeological verifiability.

The Annals of the World

First published in Latin in 1654 and then English in 1658, *The Annals of the World* is a 1,600-page volume authored by Dr. James Ussher, and is considered one of the classic works of literature that is respected for its diligence and accuracy. More precisely in Latin, this literature was called *Annales Veteris Testamenti, a prima mundi origine deducti* (*Annals of the Old Testament, deduced from the first origins of the world*). In his historic work, Dr. Ussher calculated the date of Creation to have been on October 23, 4004 BC. It was also in the seventeenth century that Dr. John Lightfoot, Vice Chancellor of Trinity College at Cambridge University, calculated the same date of Creation.[16]

Dr. James Ussher (1581–1656), was a prolific scholar and theologian. At age thirteen, he entered Trinity College Dublin (in its founding class of 1594). By age twenty, he was ordained a deacon and priest in the Anglican Church at Dublin. At age twenty-six, he was appointed chairman of the department of divinity at Dublin University. He was a professor from 1607-1621 and was twice appointed Vice Chancellor of Trinity College at the University of Dublin. He was appointed Archbishop of Ireland between 1625 and 1656. In 1628, King James I of England and Ireland, appointed Dr. Ussher to his Privy Council in Ireland.

Dr. Ussher was an expert in Semitic languages and vigorously argued for the reliability of the Hebrew text in the Old Testament.[17] His revised

---

[16] Religious Tolerance, Estimate of the Age of Earth.

[17] The Annals of the World, (Masters Books, Green Forest, AR, 2006), 891.

chronology of the date of Creation was included in King James Version Bibles for about 150 years until the middle of the nineteenth century. Over time, Dr. Ussher's chronology came under increasing attack from supporters of uniformitarianism (universal natural laws in geology) who claimed a much more ancient earth.

Many theologians also questioned Dr. Ussher's research, criticizing him for drawing chronological inferences from genealogical tables. However, some leading academics, such as Professor James Barr of Oxford University, argue that any professor of Hebrew or Old Testament at any world-class university would believe the figures in Genesis genealogies to provide a simple addition, a chronology from the beginning of the world up to later stages in the biblical story.[18]

While many scientists, scholars, and theologians refute Ussher's research to establish a timeline of human history, the research was nevertheless a major scholarly pursuit. Many notable scholars, including the Venerable Bede, an English monk, supported the methods and origin date conclusions of Dr. Ussher. Bede wrote in AD 723 that the dawn of humanity was 3952 BC.

Many other contemporaries of Dr. Ussher came to similar origin date conclusions, including French theologian and scholar Joseph Justus Scaliger (3949 BC), German mathematician and astronomer Johannes Kepler (3993 BC), and English physicist and mathematician, Isaac Newton (circa 4000 BC).[19], [20]

Notwithstanding evidence to the contrary, many scientists, scholars, and others continue to heavily criticize Ussher as naïve, ignorant,

---

[18] James Barr, Why the World Was Created in 4004 BC (Bulletin of the John Rylands University Library of Manchester), 575–608.

[19] Scribd. Dating Creation

[20] Jonathan Sarfati. Archbishop's Achievement. Creation Ministries International.

anti-science, and someone who based his research solely on the Bible. After extensive detailed investigation, the late Harvard paleontologist Stephen Jay Gould disagreed, saying that the archbishop's critics are not only ignorant, but they entirely misunderstood his work.[21] By all accounts, Dr. Ussher was a prolific scholar and researcher. Over 10,000 items from his personal library were bequeathed to the University of Dublin upon his death.

His colossal work contains over 12,000 footnotes from secular sources and another 2,000 references from the Bible. Just one-sixth of his research was from biblical sources. Dr. Ussher's biblical research provided the only continuous history from creation down to the death of Nebuchadnezzar of Babylon in 562 BC. The rest of Ussher's research came from his in-depth study of Chaldean, Persian, Greek, and Roman history, representing virtually all the ancient history known in Europe at the time. He was also an expert in the Bible, biblical languages, astronomy, ancient calendars, and chronology. His dating of other historical events, such as the deaths of Alexander in 323 BC and Julius Caesar in 44 BC, are in accordance with modern-day estimates.

Ussher's aim was to use ancient histories to construct a continuous timeline for all human civilization, not just a history of the Jewish nation. His scholarship was based on all known historic documents that represented the best available accounts of significant cultural events, all of which he painstakingly correlated to build a cohesive whole. Since more than 80 percent of his research was not based on biblical history, his account is not solely based on religious authority.

His working assumption was that the Bible was accurate, an assumption that has been overwhelmingly supported by archaeological evidence

---

[21] Jerry Bergman, James Ussher and His Chronology: Reasonable or Ridiculous, (ICR).

uncovered during the past four centuries since the first publication of his ground-breaking *Annals of the World*. Since there are no eye-witness accounts of the period preceding humans, Dr. Ussher's literal interpretation of the Bible can certainly be seen as reasonable and pragmatic.[22]

Irish Chronicles

Among the ancient European people were the warlike Celts; muscular, light-haired nomads who probably came from the region of Scythia. Many researchers believe the Celts were the first inhabitants of Europe after the great flood in the time of Noah. The Celts were of the Caucasian race which included ancient people of Assyria, Babylon, Persia, Scythia, Parthian, Arabia, Israel, Syria, Turkey, Afghanistan, and the Hindu region of India.

For one thousand years up until around AD 500, Celtic tribes inhabited the countries afterwards called Germany, Czech Republic, Switzerland, Gaul (France), Italy, Spain, Britain, and Ireland. Subsequently, these European colonists settled in the United States of America, Australia, and other parts of the world. The Celts also founded the ancient kingdom of Galatia, the same people addressed by St. Paul's Epistle to the Galatians.

The Celts in medieval times had an oral tradition, and the stories of kings, chieftains, and heroes were passed from generation to generation. Since there was little written history about Ireland prior to the fifth century AD, chroniclers and genealogists eventually wrote this history based on old traditional stories.

The various forms of the *Irish Chronicles* represent major sources of history for Irish society. The *Chronicles* are largely annalistic (annals) and written in a form divided in years. The *Chronicles* recorded the

---

[22] Michael Smith, Spiritual Meanderings Essay, 2010.

deaths of ecclesiastical and lay persons, battles, and unusual events, providing a glimpse of high society life.

Initially written in Latin and increasingly in Irish, the accounts were based on oral traditions and written in a repetitive and somewhat artificial chronicle style which was shared by scholars of the day. Since the Irish annals all survived in manuscripts, it has been challenging for scholars to determine which texts related to which chronicles and to what degree the evidence reflected reality at the time.

Nevertheless, despite contradictions that may exist between legends, documented history, and archeological findings, modern scholars use the *Irish Chronicles* as a prime source for historical narratives of the political and ecclesiastical centers in Ireland.

Lebor Gabála Érenn (*The Book of the Taking of Ireland*), a compilation of medieval poems and writings by an anonymous eleventh century writer, is considered a type of quasi-history. It is based on facts and legends that traces the ancestry of the Irish back to before Noah. It tells of a series of invasions of Ireland with the last invasion being the Gauls or Milesians. For six centuries, *Lebor Gabála Érenn*, including its five revisions, has survived in more than a dozen medieval manuscripts. It has proven to be enormously popular with the Irish people and influential in understanding Ireland's ancestry.

Some scholars chide these medieval recordings as nothing more than Christian writers attempting to provide the Irish with a written history comparable to the Israelites, and their provisioning of history in the Old Testament. Other scholars consider these narratives to be accurate, and question the motives of others and their anti-Christian beliefs. In his English translated book, *Irish Texts Society (1938)*, archaeologist R.A. Stewart Macalister was particularly dismissive of genuine historical detail in *Lebor Gabála Érenn*.

Other scholars such as T.F. O'Rahilly (1883-1953), suggested that the assaults on Ireland were in fact based on actual migrations or invasions. Twentieth century British poet, Robert Graves (1895-1985), argued that the depicted legends were accurately transmitted by word of mouth and the documented traditions are archaeologically plausible.

Texts related to the invasion by the Milesians were concerned with the deeds of Irish heroes and mainly in the provinces of Leinster and Munster. These texts revealed strong links between Ireland and the Irish-speaking community in Scotland. This recorded history was filled with professional warriors, hunters, and fighting among and between families.

Another medieval source of Irish history was *Foras Feasa ar Éirinn (1983)*, written by seventeenth century Irish historian Geoffrey Keating. The *Foras Feasa ar Éirinn* traced the history of Ireland from the creation of the world to the invasion of Ireland by the Normans in the twelfth century. This literature was also based on rich narrative, historical traditions, poetry, annals, and religious records. The *Forsa Feasa* was only circulated in manuscript, as Ireland's Protestant English administration would not give authority for its publication because of its pro-Catholic views.

Yet another rich source of Irish history is the 900-page *Irish Pedigrees, The Origin and Stem of the Irish Nation*, written in 1876 by Irish genealogist John O'Hart. In compiling his genealogies about ancient and medieval history, O'Hart substantively referenced the *Annals of the Four Masters*. For modern history extending beyond the seventeenth century, O'Hart referred to research by Bernard Burke, John Collins, and others. In his *Irish Pedigrees,* O'Hart presented the legendary origins of the Irish people from Adam and Eve, through to the kings of ancient Ireland. O'Hart believed in a literal interpretation of Gaelic and biblical history. He claimed that ancestry of the Irish race traced back from Milesius, a legendary Spanish king who was believed to be the thirty-sixth descendent of Adam.[23]

It is, however, *Annals of the Four Masters* that became the most extensive of all the compilations of the ancient annals of Ireland. The principle compiler of the Four Masters was Franciscan Brother Michael O'Clery, a native of Donegal, a convent in Ireland. Born circa 1590, he appears to have followed a military career in the Spanish Netherlands before joining the friars.

"It was at the secluded convent of Donegal that the learned friar commenced writing beginning the 22nd of January 1632, and concluding on the 10th of August 1636. Scarcely one of the ancient books which he brought together has survived to the present day. He spent eleven-years traveling from his base in Donegal to various religious locations and educational centers throughout Ireland, compiling genealogies of the saints and kings of Ireland. He produced a new *Lebor Gabala* (The Book of Invasions), which was previously the standard account for Ireland's early history. These annals, written in a very archaic and difficult to understand language, give us the genealogies and reigns of not only the high-kings of Ireland, but also of the provincial kings, chiefs, and heads of distinguished families, men of science, historians, poets, etc., with their respective dates given as accurately as the Four Masters could give them.

"They record the demise and succession of monarchs, saints, abbots, bishops, and ecclesiastical dignitaries. They tell of the creation and demise of countless churches, castles, abbeys, convents, and religious institutions. They give meagre details of battles, murders, tribal wars, wars with foreigners, battles with Norsemen, Normans, and English, and political changes. The facts and dates recorded by the Four Masters are

---

[23] John O'Hart, Irish Pedigrees, (James, Duffy and Co. Ltd., Dublin, Ireland), 12-17.

not their own facts and dates. From the confused mass of very ancient material, the Four Masters laboriously drew forth their dates and synchronized their facts as much as possible.

"The *Annals of the Four Masters* has been published at least in part, three times. However, they are now always read in the edition of the great Irish scholar, John O'Donovan. In this splendid work, the Irish text is given with a translation into English and a mass of the most valuable notes, topographical, genealogical, and historical contained in seven great quarto volumes. As long as Irish history exists, the Four Masters will be read in O'Donovan's translation, and the name of O'Donovan will be inseparably connected with that of O'Clery and his three distinguished researchers."[24]

The Annals of the Four Masters was dedicated by O'Clery with the inscription: "On the 22nd January, A.D. 1632, this work was undertaken in the Convent of Donegal, and was finished in the same Convent on the 10th day of August 1636; being the eleventh year of the reign of Charles, King of England, France, Scotland, and Ireland. In every country enlightened by civilization, and confirmed therein through a succession of ages, it has been customary to record the events produced by time.

"For sundry reasons, nothing was deemed more profitable and honorable than to study and peruse the works of ancient writers, who gave a faithful account of the chiefs and nobles who figured on the stage of life in the preceding ages: that posterity might be informed how their forefathers employed their time, how long they continued in power, and how they finished their days. In consequence of your uneasiness on the general ignorance of our civil history, and of the monarchs, provincial kings, lords, and chieftains who flourished in this country through a

---

[24] The Annals of the Four Masters. Catholic Encyclopedia.

succession of ages; with equal want of knowledge of the synchronism necessary for throwing light on the transactions of each, I have informed you that I entertained hopes of joining to my own labors the assistance of antiquaries I held most in esteem for compiling a body of Annals, wherein those matters should be digested under their proper heading; judging that, should such a compilation be neglected at present, or consigned to a future time, a risk might be run that the materials for it would never again be brought together. In this idea, I have collected the most authentic Annals I could find in my travels (from 1616-1632) through the kingdom; from which I have compiled this work, which I now commit to the world under your name and patronage."[25]

Irish historian Bernadette Cunningham demonstrated in her book, *The Annals of the Four Masters (2014)*, that despite O'Clery and his researchers being influenced by the ideals of the Catholic Counter-Reformation, they nevertheless exchanged sources and information with Anglican scholars such as Archbishop James Ussher and Anglo-Irish historian, Sir James Ware (1594-1666).

A significant element of the *Chronicles of Ireland* was its record of events in northern Britain. These chronicles documented stories about the Gaelic-speaking Scots of Dál Riata, the area west of the Highlands, covering modern Argyll and the Inner Hebrides dating back to the early sixth century. The *Chronicles of Ireland* also detailed the succession of the "High Kings of Ireland," who are claimed to have had lordship over the whole of Ireland. Medieval and early modern Irish literature portrays an almost unbroken sequence of High Kings, ruling from the Hill of Tara in County Meath, Ireland (twenty-three kilometers northwest of Dublin). These High Kings ruled over a hierarchy of lesser kings, stretching back since the seventh century AD.

---

[25] The Annals of the Four Masters. Library Ireland.

"The High Kingship was not really ever a countrywide position, or at least was never accepted by the entire country at any one time. That simply was not the Celtic way. The High King was an elected position, not hereditary, which caused much havoc among those who got their way and those who didn't. For the most part of twelve centuries, the country was marked by territorial battles among separate tribes, various families, and over one-hundred small kingdoms."[26]

Several manuscript copies of the *Chronicles* are today held at the Royal Irish Academy, the National Library of Ireland, University College, and Trinity College at the University of Dublin.

While science can corroborate much of our understanding of recorded history, it cannot prove the authenticity or accuracy of these ancient and medieval writings. The most rational and reasonable method to connect Adam to Queen Elizabeth II is to consider the evidence and develop a predominant philosophy that considers the thought and reasoning for what has been discovered, discerned, and determined. The idea of connecting Adam to Queen Elizabeth II, and to all of humankind for that matter, is a big idea that demands a considerable philosophy by which this narrative can be told. *The Adam Connection* narrative requires a philosophy, an approach that assesses the truth and meaning of certain theories or beliefs in terms of their practical application. That philosophy is pragmatism.

---

[26] Malachy McCourt, History of Ireland, (Running Press, Philadelphia, PA 19103), 50.

A New Map of North America From the Latest Discoveries (1778).
Courtesy the Library of Congress Geography and Map Division. This
region is where the philosophy of pragmatism originated.

Chapter 2

The Truth of Pragmatism

The final and most significant background for my research and writing *The Adam Connection*, has been to consider which philosophy would best frame this ancestral story. To practically apply my research and inform my writing, I knew that I would need to discern the many conflicting beliefs of science and religion. I became acutely mindful that perspectives from ancient and medieval history can be energizing for some and inconsequential for others.

The same biblical scholar who told me that most scientists do not believe Adam is the first man created by God, also declared that they overwhelmingly accept Darwin's theory of evolution as scientific fact. He said that this same belief system would not only apply to most scientists, but also to most of the world's population. I remember being rather confused by his disclosure, and then he went on to ask me a simple question.

What is your philosophy for continuing your research and writing this story?

After asking the question and observing my bewilderment, he professionally threw me a proverbial life-line to suggest I start with a noted Christian philosopher that may provide some helpful insights.

I did learn more from that Christian philosopher, but I still did not have that overarching philosophy that would become an equivalent "scientific-method" to guide my research and storytelling. Then I remembered a book in my library that an academic scholar from Washington D.C. had suggested to me over twenty years earlier. That book was about a nineteenth century philosopher named William James, and his essays about pragmatism and the meaning of truth. Within these pages, I found my philosophy.

The philosophy of pragmatism was a uniquely American perspective that evolved within a generation following Darwin's theory that had quickly shaken the foundation of religious and scientific scholarship in 1859.

When I uncovered the six-thousand-year connection between Adam and Queen Elizabeth, it never occurred to me that science and religion would be so contradictory with respect to beliefs, truths, and practical consequences of humankind ancestry. While some people hang tightly to the irreconcilable clash between science and religion, I believe it is pragmatism that can guide us toward compatibility and not competition. It is pragmatism that can guide us to the truth about our personal beliefs.

It is pragmatism that can guide in the practical application of ancient and medieval history, and help me tell this ancestry story.

What Is Pragmatism?

The Stanford Encyclopedia of Philosophy defines pragmatism as a philosophical tradition that originated in the United States in 1870. Charles Sanders Peirce (1839-1914) was the first person to term the word "pragmatism." Pierce was an American philosopher, mathematician, and scientist who was educated as a chemist and employed as a scientist for thirty years. Today, he is appreciated largely for his contributions to logic, mathematics, philosophy, and the scientific method.[27]

Pierce was followed by one of the most important of the classical pragmatists, Harvard professor William James (1842–1910). William James was an American philosopher and psychologist, who was also trained as a physician. He was the first educator to offer a psychology course in the United States, and was considered one of the leading thinkers of the late nineteenth century. Many consider William James to be one of the most influential philosophers the United States has ever produced.

Pragmatists consider thought as a tool for prediction, problem solving, and action. Pragmatism argues that philosophies such as the nature of knowledge, concepts, meaning, belief, and science are all best understood in terms of their practical uses and successes.

The core of pragmatism is clarifying the contents of a hypothesis and then tracing its "practical" consequence. In the work of James, the most influential application of pragmatism was for the concept of truth.

While pragmatism started out simply as a theory of meaning, it quickly expanded to have wide-ranging implications for the philosophy of science, logic, metaphysics (fundamental nature of being and

---

[27] Christopher Hookway, Pragmatism, Stanford Encyclopedia of Philosophy. 2013.

the world), aesthetics, logical positivism, sociology, public administration, feminism, ordinary language, and religion.

James believed that pragmatism would show us the way to overcome the irreconcilable clash between two ways of thinking about things, such as the claims of science on one hand with those of religion and morality on the other. Philosophically, he observed there is a natural clash of human temperaments between the tough-minded and the tender-minded.

Tough-minded people tend to have an empirical commitment to experience and going by the facts, while the tender-minded are inclined towards principles which appeal to the mind. His philosophy of pragmatism went on to say that the tender-minded are inclined to be more idealistic, optimistic, and religious, while the tough-minded were normally materialistic, pessimistic, and irreligious. The tender-minded are dogmatic and the tough-minded are skeptical.

For James, pragmatism offered a way of overcoming the science and religion dilemma, offering a way of seeing how science, morality, and religion are not in competition. In his lectures on pragmatism, James presented the idea that people do not need reasons for their beliefs when there is no individual reason for that person to disbelieve. He argued that the truth of a belief or theological intention has value for life, because the idea of God possessed a majesty which can provide comfort to decent people. His philosophy of pragmatism suggested that a belief can be made true by the fact that a person's belief contributes to happiness and fulfillment. Pragmatists see themselves as returning to common sense and the facts of experience.

There are some objections to pragmatism as a philosophy that reconciles science and religion. This includes the notion of relativism, which was argued by British philosopher, mathematician, and logician, Bertrand Russell. Russell believed James' doctrine was an attempt to build a superstructure of belief upon a foundation of skepticism. The skepticism described by Dr. Russell, originated from the scientific community. As noted earlier, science and its scientific method leave no room for God, because the existence of God is unprovable.

Unshaken by such skepticism, James said, "Our fundamental ways of thinking about things are discoveries of exceedingly remote ancestors, which have been able to preserve themselves throughout the experience of all subsequent time. They form one great stage of equilibrium in the human mind's development, the stage of common sense."[28]

Therefore, pragmatism characterizes truth in terms of usefulness and acceptance.

James believed that people can construct truth while in the process of living in the world. Ideas that become truth are those that can be assimilated, validated, corroborated, and verified. Truth happens to an idea. It is made true by events. Its truth is the fact of an event, a process. It is verified. The practical value of true ideas is then primarily derived from the practical importance to us.[29]

Pragmatically, we can now tell this unexpected story of *The Adam Connection* beginning with Adam.

---

[28] William James, A New Name for Some Old Ways of Thinking, (Longman Green, New York, NY)

[29] William James, Pragmatism and the Meaning of Truth, (Harvard University Press, Cambridge, Massachusetts), 83.

Map of the Old Kingdom of Judah and Israel (1759).
Courtesy Library of Congress Geography and Map Division.
This is the region of the ancient birthplace of Adam.

Chapter 3

The Age of Creation (4004 BC)

The 144 generations of *The Adam Connection* are categorized into twelve blocks of time I call "Ages." Each age portrays a theme that transcends the people, connections, and environment of that time in history. The number twelve can be found 187 times in the Bible. It is considered a perfect number, symbolizing God's power, and authority. Four thousand years after God created Adam, Jesus Christ was born into the world. He chose twelve men to bear witness to what He did and spread the good news of the gospel to the entire world. The twelve ages of this narrative are intentional.

The Age of Creation

The book of Genesis in the Bible introduces Adam as the first man created in the image of God. In this first generation, Adam is described as exceptional and powerful, especially as compared to the other elements of God's creation. It is impossible to know what it might have been like at the dawn of Creation, but I can easily imagine that it would have been a time of awesome wonder and breathless anticipation. From time to time, all of us have experienced what it is like to see the world through the eyes of a child. We often experience this child-like wonder through our relationships with God and His Creation in nature. We also experience it through our family relationships, especially with our children or grand-children during their formative years.

**In the beginning, Adam must have experienced
God and His Creation
with this child-like wonder.**

Interestingly, the name *Adam* in Hebrew can mean many things, including description of a species, archetype, and an individual person. I would never have imagined that large populations of believers in God either do not think of Adam as a real person or never think about Adam much at all. What a mistake that is when exploring the possibilities of connecting humankind with this first human being.

The descendants of Adam and Eve in this *Age of Creation*, may be unfamiliar for many. Their stories are best considered from the perspective of original sin and a near-perfect environment that enabled long-lives. The wonderment and beauty of God's creation is contrasted with these generations who would have been the first people to murder, poly-amide, and marry within immediate families.

**Ultimately, God became so angry
with the generations in this Age,
He destroyed humanity and recreated His Kingdom
with a chosen few.**

Adam
(First Generation)

We are reminded that God vested His authority in Moses, a divinely inspired human author who wrote the book of Genesis. When we read Genesis, we are reading an ancient document and should make assumptions that are appropriate for the ancient world and yet provide profound thought for our modern day.

Bill Moyers, American Journalist and author of *Genesis, A Living Conversation (1998)*, reflected on how the first book of the Bible has inspired three of the world's enduring religions (Judaism, Christianity, Islam), and the spiritual, ethical, and literary imagination of Western civilization. Moyers said that Genesis is a story about the creation of the world, through the founding of Israel from the architecture of the cosmos. He further said there are as many methods of interpreting the Bible as there are interpreters. Each of us arrives at our own interpretation and personal belief through an intricate path that has been woven by inherited memories, experiences, convictions, doctrines, dogmas, habits, and knowledge. The timeless words in the Bible are based on the relationship between the text and the reader, and connect with all of us in today's generation.[30]

> *Then God said, "Let us make mankind in our image, in our likeness, so that they may rule over the fish in the sea and the birds in the sky, over the livestock and all the wild animals, and over all the creatures that move along the ground." So, God created mankind in his own image, in the image of God he created them; male and female he created them. God blessed them and said to them, "Be fruitful and increase in number; fill the earth and subdue*

---

[30] Bill Moyers, Genesis, A Living Conversation, (Doubleday, New York, NY), xv.

*it. Rule over the fish in the sea and the birds in the sky
and over every living creature that moves on the ground.
Then God said, "I give you every seed-bearing plant on
the face of the whole earth and every tree that has fruit
with seed in it. They will be yours for food. And to all the
beasts of the earth and all the birds in the sky and all the
creatures that move along the ground — everything that
has the breath of life in it — I give every green plant for
food." And it was so. God saw all that he had made, and
it was very good. And there was evening, and there was
morning—the sixth day.* (Genesis 1:26-31 NIV)

In this passage of scripture, it is striking that God chose to make
man in His image and not the image of any of the animals He had
made just the day before. God could have made man in the image of an
eagle, a gorilla, or a lion. These are three of the strongest, most powerful
creatures in the world, which ruled the animal kingdom with authority.
Instead, God chose to make man like Himself. He could have given man
no greater honor nor shown him any greater love.

Forming him from the dust of the ground, God created man with
infinite wisdom, patience, and tenderness. He molded a noble head, a
kind face, and a strong body. He built into man the power to see, hear,
think, talk, and remember. God breathed life into man and made him
a living being. For a moment in time the world stood still, in awe at
the majesty and mystery of God's creation of man. Since that day, the
mystery of the beginning has inspired the scientific, philosophical, and
religious minds, hearts, and souls of humanity.

As noted, science has developed its own timeline and alternate
theory about the creation of man. Science believes that the predeces-
sors of man began within the past ten million years, evolving around

two hundred thousand years ago. Based on his prolific research and analysis of biblical and secular literature available in the seventeenth century, James Ussher, Archbishop of the Church of Ireland, and Vice Chancellor of Trinity College in Dublin, pragmatically determined that Adam was born around 9 a.m. on October 23, 4004 BC. John Lightfoot, Vice Chancellor of Cambridge University affirmed the same date as the birthdate of Adam.

Adam in Hebrew means "human." Since the Hebrew language did not exist in the fourth millennium BC, Adam and Eve would have not called each other by those names. In fact, the Hebrew word for Adam was used throughout the book of Genesis to represent the original man in generic (species), personal (individual), and archetypal (representative) terms. Many theologians interpret an "archetype" as a representative or in non-personal terms. However, Old Testament scholars such as John H. Walton of Wheaton College, refer to archetype as a concept that embodies all others in the group and can well be an individual and usually is. He affirms the idea that Adam is an individual, a real person in a real past.[31]

In a literary sense, an archetype refers to a recurrent symbol or even a type of character. Unlike fictional characters who often serve as archetypes of good, evil, heroes, etc., Adam is pragmatically seen in Genesis as an individual who is also representative of a group.

Eve was the first woman and mother of humanity. She was called woman because she was taken out of man. Adam and Eve would have experienced love at first sight, instantly knowing that they belonged to each other. God fashioned man and woman as fully equal in His image. She and Adam were blessed and commissioned to rule the earth. There

---

[31] John H. Walton, *The Lost World of Adam and Eve*, (Inter Varsity Press, Downers Grove, IL), 74.

is no evidence that Eve is considered inferior or subordinate in God's design. Rather she was created as Adam's co-equal helper. She and Adam established the marriage relationship between a man and a woman. Eve was not given her name by Adam until after they ate the forbidden fruit in the Garden of Eden (Genesis 1:26-31, 2:18-23 NIV).

Rabbi Abraham J. Heschel superbly tells us about the communities of faith and the struggle of real men and women to know God.[32] History, for the storytellers of Genesis, was the unfolding of divine action and human reaction—man's search for God. Writer, professor, and widely acclaimed public speaker, Renita Weems, noted that over the centuries, our interpretation of Genesis (God, creation, and man) has developed a theology based upon chronology. She says that the relationship between men and women, beginning with Adam and Eve, reveals that they are connected. The account of Adam and Eve is a love song that finds them in one another. The man (Adam) said, "This is now bone of my bones and flesh of my flesh; she shall be called 'woman', for she was taken out of man" (Genesis 2:23 NIV).

Professor Walton sees profound messages associated with the archetype representations in Genesis. Namely, humankind was created with mortal bodies, provisioned by God, given the role of serving in sacred space, tasked to have a relationship with God, and divided into male and female in order to seek out new family relationships.

British Anglican clergyman, John Robert Walmsley Scott, a leader of the worldwide evangelical movement and author of more than fifty religious books, affirms an essential truth that God created every human being with the ability to think rationally. He notes that in Genesis, we see God communicating with man in a manner that expects cooperation, consciousness, and intelligence. God invites man to lord over the

---

[32] Abraham Joshua Heschel, Jewish Virtual Library.

animals, and He creates woman in a way that man immediately recognizes her suitability as a life partner. This basic rationality of man by Creation, is not to be taken for granted.[33]

"These are the generations of the heavens and of the earth when they were created" (Genesis 2:4 KJV). The story of Adam and Eve is central to the belief that God created human beings to live in a paradise on earth. God took a rib out of Adam's side while he slept and fashioned woman. The story of Genesis provides a basis for the belief that humanity is a single family with everyone descended from an original pair of ancestors.

Adam lived for 930 years and died in 3074 BC. Adam and his wife Eve had several daughters and sons, including Cain and Abel. Abel was the first shepherd who liked to work with animals. Cain would have been the first farmer because he liked to grow things. Over the course of time, Cain brought some fruit of the soil as an offering to God, as did Abel, who brought fat portions from some of the firstborn animals of his flock. It is said that God favored Abel for his offering, and Cain became so incensed by his favor from the Lord, that he brutally murdered his brother Abel. This act became the first known murder in recorded history. Anger, jealousy, and murder were birthed at the dawn of civilization and would become prevalent throughout the whole earth.

"Nevertheless, death reigned from the time of Adam to Moses, even over those who did not sin by breaking a command, as did Adam, who was a pattern of the one to come" (Romans 5:14). Evil prevailed over all humankind until the birth of Jesus Christ. By His death and resurrection, love overcame evil, and the sins of humankind were forgiven. Ancient Jewish texts say that Adam and Eve had a daughter after Abel's

---

[33] Francis S. Collins, Belief, Readings on the Reasons for Faith, (Harper Collins, New York, NY), 111.

death, Awan, and yet nine more sons. At 130 years old, Adam became father to a son named Seth.

Seth
(Second Generation)

Seth was born after Abel's murder. Eve believed God had appointed him as a replacement for Abel (Genesis 4:25). Christians believe that Seth's genealogy leads to the savior of the world, Jesus Christ. Born in 3974 BC, Seth lived to the age of 912, and died in 3072 BC. Seth married his sister, Azura, who according to the Book of Jubilees (ancient Jewish religious manuscripts), was four years younger than Seth. Seth was 105 years old when he fathered his son, Enosh.

Enosh
(Third Generation)

Enosh was born in 3769 BC and died at the age of 905 in 2864 BC. Also known by the names Enos and Enoch, Enosh denotes man as frail and mortal. The origin of the name Enosh is Aramaic and means man or mankind. Enosh was the first son of Seth and was the first man of humankind to begin calling upon the name of God (Genesis 4:26). The ATS Bible Dictionary says that organized and systematic public worship began with Enosh, for the purpose of marking the distinction between men of God and the ungodly.[34] He married his sister, Noam and she bore Barakiel, and at age ninety, Enosh became father to their son, Cainan or Keinan.

---

[34] Enosh. Bible Hub.

Cainan
(Fourth Generation)

Cainan was born in 3679 BC and was 910 years old when he died in 2769 BC. His name in Greek is Kainan and in Hebrew his name is Keinan, which possibly means possession. He married his sister, Mualeleth. Cainan was seventy years old when Mualeleth bore their son, Mahalalel.

Mahalalel
(Fifth Generation)

Mahalalel was born in 3365 BC and died at the age of 895 in 2470 BC. He married Dinah, daughter of Barakiel, the daughter of his father's brother. Their children were Danel and at the age sixty-five, Mahalalel fathered a son, Jared.

Jared
(Sixth Generation)

Jared was born in 3300 BC and died at the age of 962 in 2338 BC. His wife was Baraka, the daughter of Rasujal, a daughter of his father's brother. Their first child was Azrial, and at the age of 162, Jared fathered a son, Enoch.

Enoch
(Seventh Generation)

Enoch was born in 3135 BC and died at the age of 365 in 2770 BC. Enoch was the first among men born on earth who learned writing, knowledge, and wisdom. He saw and understood everything and was favored in the eyes of God. His wife was Edna, the daughter of Danel, the daughter of his father's brother. Enoch and Edna had children named Barakil, Naamah, and their son, Methuselah.

Methuselah
(Eighth Generation)

Methuselah was born in 3070 BC and died at the age of 969 in 1656 BC. Methuselah in Hebrew means "Man of the spear." He is the longest living person in recorded history. The name of Methuselah today is synonymous for any old or long-lasting person. One of the most famous people in biblical history, Methuselah was the grandfather of Noah. His wife was Edna, daughter of Azrial, the daughter of his father's brother.[35] He is believed to have died seven years before the great flood. Methuselah had other sons and daughters with Edna, before he fathered Lamech when he was 187 years old.

Lamech
(Ninth Generation)

Lamech was born in 2,886 BC and died at the age of 777 in 2109 BC. *Smith's Bible Dictionary* reports that Lamech had two wives, Adah and Zillah. His daughter Naamah, along with Eve, are the only ancient women whose names are mentioned by Moses. From his marriage to Zillah, Lamech fathered their children Tubal-Cain, and Naamah. From his marriage with Adah, he fathered sons, Jabal, Jubal, and Noah.

Tubal-cain, Jabal, and Jubal are celebrated in scripture as authors of useful inventions. Tubal-cain is believed to have invented the sword

---

[35] The Book of Jubilees, Chapter 4:1-27

and in this possession, Lamech foresaw great advantage to his family over any enemies.

Lamech himself was skilled in agriculture, music, and several mechanical arts. He was the first to violate the primeval ordinance of marriage (Genesis 4:18-24) and is the first polygamist in recorded history. Known for his blustering tyranny and braggadocio, Lamech did not put his trust in God, but in weapons and inventions by his sons that enhanced the physical and material powers of man.

Lamech was 182 years old when he and Adah had another son, Noah, from which the entire world's population has descended.

Turkey in Asia Drawn from the Most Respectable Authorities (1817).
This is the ancient region where Noah and his family settled
after the "Great Flood".

Chapter 4

The Age of Re-Creation (2704 BC)

———※———

This second period covers one generation over more than 250 years. It is a dramatic account of Noah and what I am calling The Age of Re-Creation. The Age of Creation that began with Adam and his descendants would become transformed with the birth of a man named Noah.

The account of Noah, the Ark, and the great flood is one of the best-known stories in the Bible. Children of God have enjoyed this enchanting story for over 2,000 years. The pairing of all living animals, birds, and creatures that boarded the Ark seems to have captured the imagination of humankind. Many believe this story is a literal account, while others are either unsure, skeptical, or unbelieving. On the other hand, the identity and ancestral connections from Noah, his wife, sons, and their wives seem to be less known and relatively unimportant.

Paradoxically, it is the ancestry of Noah and his family that profoundly connects humankind.

However, the belief by most scientists is that Noah and his family are just men, women, and children who evolved over 2,000 years as members of the Homo-sapiens species. As my research continued and I laid aside any of my potential preconceived beliefs about the origin of man, I found myself increasingly uninspired by an evolution theory and more hopeful about a connection theory that can be traced back to Noah and this Age of Re-Creation.

My investigations also came across modern day researchers who identified what seems to be the location of the remains of an Ark that supports the existence of a great flood and the vessel in the Noah story. I also note that the movie, *Is Genesis History*, also seems to provide compelling scientific evidence of a great flood that would have occurred in the timeframe consistent with *The Adam Connection* narrative. Interestingly, I discussed this research with an academic scholar who reminded me that skeptics will likely be unconvinced by such "proof." His wise counsel affirmed to me that everyone has preconceived beliefs, and it is belief that determines a personal truth.

I believe the Age of Re-Creation was the new beginning after Adam.

Noah
(Tenth Generation)

> *Then the Lord said to Noah, "Enter the Ark, you and all your household, for you alone I have seen to be righteous before Me in this time." (Genesis 7:1 NIV)*

Noah was born in 2704 BC and died at age 950 in 1754 BC, at Mount Ararat, Turkey. Mt. Ararat is in Eastern Turkey on the borders of modern day Iran and Armenia. Mt. Ararat is a 17,000 feet high volcanic mountain, towering above the surrounding plains. The earliest reference to Noah's Ark landing on Mt. Ararat was around AD 425 by the early church historian, Philostorgius.

The story of Noah's Ark and the Great Flood seems to have been affirmed by acclaimed underwater archaeologist, Robert Ballard, who believes he found proof that the biblical flood was based on real events. In an interview with Christiane Amanpour for ABC News, Ballard, talked about his findings. His team probed the depths of the Black Sea off the coast of Turkey in search of traces of an ancient civilization hidden underwater since the time of Noah. His finding seemed to confirm that the region around Mt. Ararat may very well be the birthplace from which all the people of the world are derived. This place would have then become the cradle of humanity, and the focal point for the subsequent dispersion of all humankind.[36]

Accounts of massive floods are found in many cultures around the world including, *The Gilgamesh Epic*, a saga of an ancient Babylonia King, recorded on a series of baked clay tablets. The Epic of Gilgamesh, a poem from ancient Mesopotamia, is considered one of the earliest surviving great works of literature. Noah was a preacher, Ark builder, husband, and father. Noah, which means "rest," was named so by his family as comfort for the difficult times the old world was experiencing due to generational unrighteousness. Noah was called to provide comfort for the whole world, which needed divine relief and leadership by a comforting person.

---

[36] J. Millman, B. Taylor and L. Effron, Evidence Noah's Biblical Flood Happened says Robert Ballard. ABC News.

Noah was a man of high moral character. He was pure, decent, and civil in contrast to his peers who were perverse and hateful characters. The Bible says that the world at that time was corrupt and full of violence, yet Noah found grace in the eyes of the God. He was chosen for a very special purpose. "Noah found favor in the eyes of the Lord" (Genesis 6:9 NIV). Noah was 600 years old when he and his family stepped on the Ark after building it for about 100 years.

Then the Lord said to Noah, "Go into the ark, you, and your whole family, because I have found you righteous in this generation. Take with you the seven others of this generation. Take with you two of every kind of clean animal, a male and its mate, and two of every kind of bird, male and female, to keep their various kinds alive throughout the earth. Seven days from now I will send rain on the earth for forty days and forty nights, and I will wipe from the face of the earth, every living creature I have made, and also seven pairs of every kind of bird, male and female, to keep their various kinds alive throughout the earth." Noah did all that the Lord commanded him.

Noah was six hundred years old when the floodwaters came on the earth. Noah, his sons, his wife, and his sons' wives entered the ark to escape the waters of the flood. Pairs of clean and unclean animals, of birds and of all creatures that move along the ground, male and female, came to Noah and entered the ark, as God had commanded Noah. After the seven days, the floodwaters came on the earth. In the six hundredth year of Noah's life, on the seventeenth day of the second month—on that day all the springs of the great deep burst forth, and the floodgates of the heavens were opened. Rain fell on the earth forty days and forty nights. On that very day Noah and his sons, Shem, Ham, and Japheth, together with his wife and the wives of his three sons, entered the ark.

They had with them every wild animal according to its kind, all livestock according to their kinds, every creature that moves along the ground according to its kind, and every bird according to its kind, everything with wings. Pairs of all creatures that have the breath of life in them came to Noah and entered the ark. The animals going in were male and female of every living thing, as God had commanded Noah. Then the Lord shut him in. For forty days, the flood kept coming on the earth, and as the waters increased they lifted the ark high above the earth.

The waters rose and increased greatly on the earth, and the ark floated on the surface of the water. They rose greatly on the earth, and all the high mountains under the entire heavens were covered. The waters rose and covered the mountains to a depth of more than fifteen cubits (22 ½ feet). Every living thing that moved on land perished—birds, livestock, wild animals, all the creatures that swarm over the earth, and all mankind. Everything on dry land that had the breath of life in its nostrils died. Every living thing on the face of the earth was wiped out; people and animals and the creatures that move along the ground and the birds were wiped from the earth. Only Noah was

> *left, and those with him in the ark. The waters flooded the*
> *earth for a hundred and fifty days.* (Genesis 7:1-24 NIV)

After seven days of loading the Ark, forty days of underground waters bursting forth, rain falling for forty days and nights, and another 110 days of the water covering all the earth, everything became still. At this point, the water had covered the earth for 150 days. God did not forget Noah, his family, and the animals on the Ark. God sent a wind across the water and the waters began to subside. He made the waters go down and the Ark rested on the Ararat Mountain.

For another forty-days the water lowered, the mountain tops were seen, and Noah checked the water. He sent a raven and dove out of the window of the Ark every seven days until after twenty-eight days, one of the doves returned with an olive leaf, flew away, and did not return. Noah celebrated his 601st birthday and opened the roof of the Ark to see if the earth was almost dry. God told Noah the animals, birds, and every living creature could leave the Ark to reproduce and live all over the earth.

When Noah and his family stepped out of the Ark, they were the only people left on Earth. Then God blessed Noah and his sons, saying to them, "Be fruitful and increase in number and fill the earth. The fear and dread of you will fall upon all the beasts of the earth and all the birds of the air, upon every creature that moves along the ground, and upon all the fish of the sea, they are given into your hands. Everything that lives and moves will be food for you. Just as I gave you the green plants, I now give you everything" (Genesis 9:1-3 NIV).

Noah and his family were left to repopulate the Earth through children that were born to them after the flood.

Then God said to Noah and to his sons with him, "I now establish my covenant with you and with your descendants after you and with every living creature that was with you—the birds, the livestock and all the wild animals, all those that came out of the ark with you—every living creature on earth. I establish my covenant with you: Never again will all life be destroyed by the waters of a flood; never again will there be a flood to destroy the earth." And God said, "This is the sign of the covenant I am making between me and you and every living creature with you, a covenant for all generations to come: I have set my rainbow in the clouds, and it will be the sign of the covenant between me and the earth. Whenever I bring clouds over the earth and the rainbow appears in the clouds, I will remember my covenant between me and you and all living creatures of every kind. Never again will the waters become a flood to destroy all life. Whenever the rainbow appears in the clouds, I will see it and remember the everlasting covenant between God and all living creatures of every kind on the earth." God said to Noah, "This is the sign of the covenant I have established between me and all life on the earth." (Genesis 9:9-17 NIV)

According to Jewish tradition, Noah was married to his cousin Naamah, the sister of Tubal-cain, a descendant of Cain, the son of Adam and Eve. Noah and Naamah's children included Ham, Shem, and Japheth.

Ham was founder of the African continent including Syria, Arabia, and Africa. Ham was physically gifted and his descendants had an innate ability to operate physically in the natural realm. It is said that

Ham founded fourteen generations of the world's first civilizations. His grandson, Nimrod, led construction of the Tower of Babel, a massive structure so tall and offensive that God confounded the speech of everyone so they could not understand each other. The people then spread to all corners of the earth speaking different languages.

Shem was founder of the Asian continent within the Euphrates to the Indian Ocean and was considered the blessed one. Many anointed men and women descended from Shem including the first patriarch of Judaism, Abraham and Moses, author of the book of Genesis. Jesus Christ, the only begotten son of God, is also from the lineage of Shem. Exactly twenty-six Semitic nations are recorded as descending from Shem. Many languages evolved from Shem's ancestry including Hebrew, Arabic, Aramaic, Phoenician, and Akkadian.

Japheth was founder of the European continent and the rest of Asia beyond the Euphrates and was considered the thinking man. Japheth's name has meanings such as "fair, bright, and enlarge." God knew that a vast Western civilization would rise on earth from the descendants of Japheth. Fourteen nations are recorded as descending from Japheth. This includes the Greek and Roman civilizations which so profoundly impacted the history of the medieval and modern world. Many conquered people, nations, and cultures have been absorbed and integrated by Japheth's children, including all the great nations in Europe, North America, and Australasia. Noah's sixteen grandsons were heads of their family clans, which became large populations in the areas in which they resided. Some areas of the world named after Noah's ancestors include Galatia (Turkey), Gaul (France, parts of Belgium, western Germany, and northern Italy), Scythia (Romania and Ukraine), Medes (Persia, Iran, and India), Javan (Greece), Canaan (Palestine), and Aram (Syria).

Antique map of Scythia and Serik by Christoph Cellarius (1686). This region in Central Eurasia, north and northwest of the Black Sea, is the birthplace of our earliest ancestors that would go on to populate and expand the regions of India, Europe, North America, and Australasia.

Chapter 5

The Age of Repopulation (2447 BC)

By the grace of God, Noah was chosen to provide divine relief from corruption and violence for the whole world. Noah could not have known that such relief would be temporary because of the sinful nature of man. Nevertheless, he became the father from which the world repopulated.

This next Age of Repopulation is a three-generation story of Noah's son Japheth and his early descendants. In less than two centuries, these generations would become founders of people and places that would have an amazing impact on the history of civilization. The Japhethites would become known as the "Gentiles," thereby representing anyone not of Jewish faith. The Gentiles became the people and nations from which spread the gospel of Jesus Christ and advancement of Christianity in the world.

Japheth, which has been translated as "May God Enlarge," is the story of a gentle father from whom would originate and expand the Indo-European nations. The birth of the region of Scythia and origin of the tribe known as the Gaels, would evolve from the family of Japheth. The Scottish and Irish Celts along with the ancient nations of Assyria, Persia, and Babylonia would also develop from the descendants of Japheth. His descendants would go on to populate and expand the regions of India, Europe, North America, and Australasia over a period of five-thousand years after his birth.

We will learn that God did in fact enlarge the territory or geography of Japheth. However, the etymology of the word "enlarge" is from the Hebrew word *Pathah*. In this instance, *Pathah*, would be translated as "entice" or "persuade." Some scholars seem to infer that when a person is enticed or persuaded, then their original opinions would have changed, and their mind would have been opened to new thoughts and ideas. It is not a reach to consider that Japheth and his descendants would become the founders of intellectually curious nations that would explore new thoughts, ideas, and principles of science.

The Japhethites would become the thinkers of their time. The Greek and Roman philosophers were some of the most influential thinkers the world has ever known. Democracy was produced from the bloodline of Japheth. Europe would later become one of the principle contributors to the growth and maturity of philosophy, science, and religion.

Japheth of Scythia
(Eleventh Generation)

Japheth was the oldest son of Noah, born in 2447 BC, one-hundred years before the flood. His descendants inhabited the region from the ancient Taurus and Amanus mountains in eastern Turkey; eastward towards China and Russia and along Europe to the southern tip of Spain. His family lived north of the Black Sea in an area the Greeks called Scythia, which is the ancient name for the region which today includes parts of Romania and Ukraine.

The name "Scythian" was applied to those nations who displayed skill in hunting and use of the bow and arrow. The word Scythian is derived from the Celtic word "Sciot," which signifies a dart or arrow. Scythian neighbors were frequently called archers, shooters, and hunters by the names "Scythi," "Shuten" or "Schuten," each of which signifies Scythians, the name applied to the whole nation. This ancient word is still preserved in the English, German, Lithuanian, Finnish, and Lapponian (Finland), Livonian and Courlandish (Latvia), Estonian, and Prussian (Germany) languages. A fact which strongly supports that all these nations are of Scythian origin.

Historians have provided contradictory accounts with respect to the character of Scythians. At one time, Scythians have been represented as just and moderate, and at other times, they have been represented as a fierce and barbarous nation prone to cruel and shocking behavior. These contrarian accounts provide evidence that those different characteristics are to be applied to different nations in this vast family.

According to second century Latin historian Justin, the Scythians lived in great simplicity and innocence. The Scythians only gave goods and riches to someone who had attributes of strength, bravery, work ethic, liberty, goodness, and hatred of fraud and dishonesty. Herodotus, the fifth century BC Greek historian, wrote much of the earliest recorded history about Scythia, noting that the Scythians prospered economically, politically, and militarily in a widespread Middle Eastern and Asia kingdom.

During that time, the Scythians grew grain, and shipped wheat, flocks, and cheese to Greece and succeeded famously in driving back an army of 700,000, led by king Darius the Great of Persia. Jewish historian Josephus claimed in the first century AD, that the Scythians were descended from Magog. Eighteenth century French historian Charles Rollin, said, "When we compare the manners of the Scythians with those of the present age, we are tempted to believe that the pencils which drew so beautiful a picture of them were not free from

partiality; and that Justin and Horace have decked them with virtues that did not belong to them. But all antiquity agrees in giving
the same testimony of them; and Homer (Greek philosopher) whose
opinion ought to be of great weight, calls them "the most just and
upright of men."[37]

The Scythians were among the most warlike and valiant people of
antiquity, and fought chiefly in war chariots. They were expert horsemen,
and were one of the earliest people to master the art of riding and using
horse-drawn covered wagons. The Scythians were remarkable for not
only their fighting ability, but also for the complex cultures they created.

Scythian women are said to have fought alongside their men in battles of war. Scythians worshipped the sun, moon, and winds, and their
god of war, called by the Greeks "Ares" and "Odin" by the Germans
and Scandinavians. The ancestors of the Irish, Scottish, English, Polish,
Scandinavians, Germans, French, and many other ancient tribes, were
all powerful nations of the Scythians.

After some two-thousand years, in the fifth century BC, a descendant class of Chieftains, the Royal Scyths, established themselves as
rulers of the southern Russia and Crimean territories. It is from these
locations that some of the richest and numerous relics of the Scythian
civilization have been found. The Scythians worked in a variety of materials including wood, leather, bone, bronze, iron, silver, and gold. The
decorative objects produced by the ancient Scythians were generally
small in size, and superbly made of precious materials.

A reasonably clear picture has emerged in which a single family beginning with Japheth multiplied and populated the northern shore of the
Mediterranean, the whole of Europe, the British Isles, Scandinavia, and
the larger part of Russia. The same family settled India, displacing a prior

---

[37] The Scythians. Library Ireland.

Indus Valley settlement of Hamites, who descended from Japheth's brother Ham. It is possible that some of Japheth's ancestors immigrated to areas in Polynesia and Ainu in northern Japan.

Noah had said that God would enlarge Japheth (Genesis 9:27) and it seems that this enlargement continued in every part of the world except for the Far East. This enlargement did not mean that Japheth descendants were the first to migrate, but wherever they did spread and settle, they had a profound significance in the development of civilization, including areas such as ancient Greece and Rome. There are many lines of evidence that the names in Genesis 10:1-5 were indeed real people whose families carried with them clear recollections of their respective forebears, and unmistakable relationship with the patriarchal name.[38]

According to evangelical Christian pastor and author Ray Stedman, the Japhetic people are generally considered the peoples of India and Europe.[39] Most people in the United States likely descended from the Japhetic family. Japhetic people settled the entire Western hemisphere, and the Indians (Hindus) are of the same stock. There is also much to suggest in history that the enlargement that was promised to Japheth by his father Noah was also intellectual. Historically, all the great philosophers are Japhetic. The Greeks, who began modern philosophy, are descendants of Japheth, as are the Hindus, both representing the two truly great philosophic races of earth.

A study of Japheth, his sons, and grandsons reveals some light on who his descendants are today:

---

[38] Arthur C. Custance, Noah's Three Sons, (Doorway Publications, Ancaster, Ontario, Canada), 78.

[39] The Three Families of Man. Ray Stedman.

Japheth	Greeks, Aryans of India
Gomer	Black Sea, Germany, and Wales
Madai	Persia, India
Javan	Greece and Cyprus
Tubal	Russian city of Tobolsk
Meshech	Russian city of (Muskovi)Moscow
Tiras	Thracians and Etruscans of Italy
Ashkenaz	Germany, Armenia, Scandinavia, Denmark, northern islands of Europe and European west coast
Ripath	Europe, Carpathians (Ukraine), Paphlagonians (Turkey)
Togarmah	Armenians, Germany, and Turkey
Elishah	Greeks
Tarshish	Spain, Carthage (Tunisia)
Kittim	Greeks, Cyprus, and Macedonia
Dodanium	Greeks, Rhodes, and Dardanelles (Turkey)
Magog	Georgia, Scythia

According to the Jewish Book of Jubilees, Japheth married Adataneses, and they had fifteen children including Gomer, Matai, Javan, Tubal, Meshech, Tiras, and Magog who were noted in the Bible.

Magog
(Twelfth Generation)

Magog was born in 2368 BC in Scythia, the time from which he and his descendants became kings. At an early period in world history, his tribe was known as the Gaels (later Gauls), an ethnolinguistic group and branch of the Celtic languages that became Irish and Scottish Gaelic. The Gaels moved westward from the borders of Europe and Asia and reached Gaul, an ancient region in Europe that corresponds to modern day France, Belgium, the southern Netherlands, southwestern Germany, and northern Italy.

The Celts, people who spoke the Celtic language and had cultural similarities, were the first inhabitants of Europe after the great flood. The Celts were of the Caucasian race, from which descended the ancient and modern European races including the Assyrians, Babylonians, Persians, Scythians, Parthians, Arabs, Jews, Syrians, Turks, Afghans, and Hindus. To these races must also be added the European colonists who have settled in America, Australia, and other parts of the world. The descendants of Magog also were among the people of Korea, Japan, Mongolia, and much of central, northern, and southern China. Other people descended from Magog include the American Indians and Intuits, who lived in Greenland, Canada, and Alaska.

Notwithstanding all the variations in color and appearance which are observable in the Caucasian, Mongolian, Ethiopian, Himalayan, and American races, God has made of one blood all nations of men and their bloodlines exist among them all.

Considered father of the Scythians, Magog could not have imagined the evolution and influence of Scythians over the next two millennia. Originally speaking without any known language, the Scythians as a race, learned to speak a dialect of the Northeastern Iranian language family. In the subsequent fifth century BC, the Scythians surged in the Middle East, overwhelming the Assyrian infantry. Along with the Babylonian and Medes empires, they formed an alliance that shattered the Assyrian Empire. These speedy Scythian warriors would develop weaponry that included barbed arrowheads, poisonous arrow tips, putrefied human blood, and dung all purposed to wreak havoc on their enemies, and hasten death and destruction.[40]

Over time, Magog's progeny became cultured in their elaborate use of golden artwork. The Scyths were among the first people to sew gold into their garments, belts, jewelry, helmets, and even adorned gold in their weapons. The Scythian descendants of Magog would develop an eye for design, especially depictions of lions, wolves, deer, leopards, eagles, and animals in deadly combat. Herodotus attested that Scythians wore tattoos as a sign of their nobility. After battle, Scythian warriors would drink the blood of the first enemy killed, and decapitate slain enemies to receive their share of the booty from the Scythian chieftain or King who led his warriors in battle. Scalps would then become sewn into the warrior cloaks and the skulls of the most respected enemies would be cut, covered with gold, and made into wine goblets. The Scythians would later become fond of marijuana and were responsible for bringing it from Central Asia to Egypt and Eastern Europe.

While the Scythian culture would disappear in the early first millennium AD, their burial grounds remain with their tradition of building huge earth mounds, up to 60 feet in height, containing the interned remains of Scythian chiefs, kings, wives, slaves, and horses. In 1898, archeologists would find 400 horses arrayed in a geometric pattern around the body of a slain warrior, and according to Herodotus, mourners in the Scythian culture would have also included murdered slaves who would be gutted, stuffed, and impaled on posts within the burial mound.[41]

---

[40] www.listverse.com, Top Interesting Facts about the Scythians.

[41] Ibid.

After the disappearance of the Scythian culture, their legacy continued most notably through the ancient Germans, Danes, Swedes, Norwegians, Dutch, Swiss, English, and Irish.

The sons of Magog included Ali, Jobhath, Elichanaf, Chalaf, Fathochta, Lubal, and Boath.

Boath
(Thirteenth Generation)

Boath was born around 2334 BC. He is described as one of the men of Scythia and the Goths' clan. Legend has it that the Goths originated far to the north on the shores and islands of what is today known as Sweden. For a time, the Goths ruled a great kingdom north of the Danube River and the Black Sea. Boath's descendants would likely have become some of the first Germanic people and within the next two millennia, would sweep into Europe and join the Huns in racial coexistence with the Roman Empire. It appears that none of Boath's descendants were involved in building the Tower of Babel, which incurred the wrath of God and dispersion of people around the world. Boath married Feninsa Farsa. Their son was Fenius.

These three generations had a tremendous impact on the creation and development of civilizations that would follow over the next forty-five hundred years. Originating in what we know today as eastern Turkey, this Age of Repopulation would spawn a royal bloodline that would become known by their inventions and nomadic expansion by land and sea. Why did these first kings come into existence? What was their sovereign purpose and how would they choose to rule? Words such as barbaric, savage, murderous, cruel, and ruthless provide a cultural backdrop for these next generations of wandering pioneers.

Antique map of the Mediterranean Sea divided into its principal parts of the seas. "To the most serene and most sacred Majesty James II by the Grace of God King of Great Brittain, France and Ireland." William Berry (1685). Courtesy Library of Congress Geography and Map Division. This region represents the migration of these generations from eastern to western Mediterranean and settlement in the Iberian Peninsula.

Chapter 6

The Age of First Kings (2300 BC)

The next twenty-two generations extend over a course of more than five-hundred years, in what I am calling the Age of First Kings. According to historical records in the *Irish Chronicles*, this is the time in ancient history that a form of bloodline monarchy developed with the naming of kings. It is difficult to say with certainty whether the men in these generations were of a royal bloodline. However, chroniclers did consider these men to be appointed monarchs, often ascending to their royal positions after battle between nations or killings within royal families.

The first and most influential king in this *Age of First Kings* was the legendary Fenius Farsa. After journeying to Babylon, the ancient city in Mesopotamia, King Fenius Farsa along with a great number of scholars, invented an alphabet that would have a profound impact on languages and the advancement of civilization in Europe and the world. Perhaps even more interesting for modern day readers, is the branch of linguistics (phonetics) that evolved from his alphabet invention. This branch became the study of the sounds of human speech, and the equivalent aspects of sign language.

The *Irish Chronicles* provided scant details about these generations, however, our research discerned that these generations of men and women were adventurers who expanded their Scythian culture throughout the Mediterranean basin, including countries that we know today as Greece, Cyprus, North Africa, Portugal, Spain, northern England, Ireland, and Scotland. As a side note, we also learned that a family member of King Fenius Farsa was a contemporary of the infant-child Moses, who went on to lead the Jewish people out of exile from Egypt.

The influential descendants of King Fenius Farsa founded the nomadic tribe known as the Gaels. Today, we know the Gaels as an ethnolinguistic group who would become known as the Gaelic speaking Celts of Ireland, Scotland, and the Isle of Man, which today is a crown dependency of the United Kingdom and located between Northern Ireland and England.

These twenty-two generations in The Age of First Kings were nomadic, migratory, and fierce invaders of new territories as they expanded westward from the Middle East, to the regions and nations of Europe, Middle East, and North Africa. Their languages profoundly influenced the cultures and civilizations of ancient, medieval, and modern history.

King Fenius Farsa
(Fourteenth Generation)

Fenius Farsa, born in 2300 BC, was King of Scythia. According to some traditions, at the time when Nimus (Nimrod) ruled the Assyrian Empire, Fenius Farsa journeyed to the Tower of Babel after its collapse. The Tower of Babel was in the ancient city of Babylon, a major city of ancient Mesopotamia. Fenius Farsa, along with seventy-two scholars and ten years of study, invented the Ogham alphabet and Gaelic language.

The name Fenius was also known as Phoeniusa. From Phoeniusa descended a race of people known as "Phoenicians," from which derived the word "phonetic," meaning a system of writing using symbols and sounds. Phoenicians were the ancestors of the Celts that later inhabited Ireland and emigrated to Scotland and England.

Many historians consider the Phoenicians to be one of the first civilized nations of the world. The civilizations of Assyria, Babylonia, Egypt, Greece, and other countries owe their origin and development to them as the Phoenicians had colonies in many countries. In ancient times, the Red Sea and the Mediterranean Sea were connected by a strait through which the Phoenician ships entered the Mediterranean and migrated to Europe.

Fenius and his scholars developed the Ogham alphabet as a perfect writing system for his languages, and the letters were named after trees or his best twenty-five scholars. A series of perpendicular and intersecting lines characterizes the Ogham alphabet. The Auraicept, a seventh century manuscript written by Irish grammarian scholar named Longarad, claims that Fenius Farsa discovered four alphabets: Hebrew, Greek, Latin, and Ogham.

The Irish language originated with the first Celtic people who arrived in Ireland in a period predating recorded history. Primitive Irish was written on stone monuments, using the medieval alphabet Ogham, between approximately the fourth and tenth centuries AD. These medieval writings are believed to be close in form to commonly spoken Celtic. Common Celtic is the ancestor of the languages spoken by the culturally similar Celtic people located throughout medieval Europe. There are roughly 400 surviving Ogham orthodox inscriptions on stone monuments throughout Ireland and western Britain.

From the fifth-century onwards, Christian influence led to what is called "Old" Irish, which appeared in writings in the margins of Latin manuscripts. By the tenth century, writings evolved into "Middle" Irish. "Classical" Irish was used between the thirteenth and eighteenth centuries. During these periods, the arrival of the Vikings, Norman, and British settlers affected the Irish language. Gaelic Ireland went into terminal decline due to a series of destructive wars and British inhabitation between the sixteenth and seventeenth centuries.

By the early nineteenth century when J. O'Brien compiled his Irish-English dictionary, Irish Gaelic speakers were in decline as Protestantism ascended and made English the dominant language of education, politics, and business. The marginalized Catholic Gaelic Irish language was decimated simultaneously by the Great Famine of the 1840s, and the growing dominance of English throughout much of the world, especially in the United States. Gaelic became increasingly seen as outmoded and redundant.

In the late nineteenth century, there was a popular renaissance of Irish nationalism and by the 1920s, Ireland had broken with the British Empire. Irish nationalists hoped to revive the language which was by then confined to pockets of the west of Ireland called Gaeltacht. Irish became the first official language of the state while Irish was made a compulsory subject in schools. It was hoped that within a generation, Ireland would become a predominantly Irish-speaking country. By the early twenty-first century, it was estimated that only between 40,000-80,000 people could still speak Irish as their first language, and many have predicted the language will soon die out entirely as a spoken language.[42]

---

[42] J. O'Brien, Irish-English Dictionary, 2nd Edition, (Hodges and Smith).

During his lifetime, Fenius married Belait Latium and their children were Esru and Niul. The descendants of Fenius Farsa became known as Feiné.

Niul Nemnach
(Fifteenth Generation)

Niul Nemnach was governor of Campus Cyrunt and Prince of Scythia. He was born around 2227 BC in the sparsely populated region of Campus Cyrunt, Egypt. After his father returned to Scythia, Niul lived for some time at Oeothena, teaching the languages and other admirable sciences. He was invited into Egypt by Pharaoh Smenkhkare, who gave him the land of Campus Cyrunt to inhabit. The ancient Irish historians tell us that the river "Nile" was named after Niul.

Niul married Scota of Egypt, daughter of Pharaoh Smenkhkare who was married to Merytaten, the daughter of Pharaoh Amenhotep IV Akhenaten and Queen Neferiti. The phonetic version of Smenkhkare is Smehkharon and this pronunciation provides the name by which history knows him best, that of Aaron, who was described in the Bible as the brother of Moses. Aaron was Moses' first cousin and a feeding brother of Moses. Aaron's mother, Tey was the woman who nursed Moses when he was born.

It is said that Niul and Scota cared for the welfare and education of Moses who enjoyed their affection and was a great friend of their son Gaodhal. We are told that Moses tried to convince Niul to go on board one of Pharaoh's ships in the Red Sea to witness the miracle performed by God in delivering the Israelites from Egyptian bondage. While Niul sympathized with the Israelites in their great affliction, he declined because he was the son-in-law of Pharaoh. Moses excused him for declining the invitation. The Feiné and Israelites maintained a friendship for a long while.

Before the migration of Niul and Scota to Ireland and Scotland, the Scythians were descended from Noah's son Japheth and some clans from Ham. Ham, also known as Thoth, is the supposed author of the *Egyptian Book of the Dead* containing the original version of the Ten Commandments. The eldest son of Niul and Scota was named Gaodhal after his namesake, who was a son of Ethor, a learned and skillful man who refined the Gaelic language.

Gaodhal Glas
(Sixteenth Generation)

Gaodhal Glas was Chieftain of the Gaels. The Gaels were a nomadic tribe that journeyed far on land and sea. Some may say that the history and migration patterns of the Gaels cannot be believed because navigation was unknown in these ancient times. These objections vanish when considering the art of sailing would have been in use at times since Noah and subsequent archaeological findings that would seem to validate the existence of his Ark.

Gaodhal was born around 2187 BC in Campus Cyrunt near the Red Sea. At that time in history, the Red Sea would have been a long, narrow, landlocked sea that separates Africa from the Arabian Peninsula and links the Mediterranean Sea to the Indian Ocean.

The *Irish Chronicles* affirm that Gaodhal and his tribe painted the figures of animals and birds on banners, shields, and other natural renderings to distinguish themselves in the same manner as the Israelites. The "Thunderbolt" became the chief standard for many generations after Gaodhal.

Gaodhal would have been a contemporary of Abraham, the God-appointed leader of the Israelites. Abraham was the first of the Hebrew patriarchs (along with Isaac and Jacob) revered by the three monotheistic religions (Judaism, Christianity, and Islam).

Gaodhal's sons were Easruth, who died in Crete, and Asruth Esru.

Asruth Esru
(Seventeenth Generation)

Asruth Esru was born in 2145 BC in Campus Cyrunt, Egypt. He died in Crete, Greece. He was Prince of Crete and an Egyptian Governor. It is likely that Asruth Esru would have been appointed an Egyptian Governor by the Pharaoh. The *Chronicles* say that he ruled in peace. As an Egyptian Governor, Asruth would have had political, economic, and administrative responsibilities for a large, perhaps lightly populated area near the Red Sea. He most likely immigrated to Crete which is the largest of the Greek islands and fifth-largest in the Mediterranean Sea. His son was Sruth.

Sruth
(Eighteenth Generation)

Sruth was born in 2122 BC in Egypt. He died in Crete. He was Prince of Crete and an Egyptian Governor. Sruth would have held another governorship position alongside his father in an area near the Red Sea. Sruth and his Feiné colony were invaded by the Egyptians on account of their affiliation with the Israelites during their release from Egyptian bondage. After many battles and conflicts, most of his colony lost their lives. The remaining few led by Prince Sruth were forced to depart the country, immigrating to the island of Candia, later known as Crete. Sailing from the area today known as Alexandria, Egypt, Sruth and his colony would have sailed the Mediterranean for a few days until they arrived in Crete. Sruth's son was Heber.

King Heber Scut
(Nineteenth Generation)

Heber Scut was King of Scythia and was born in 2100 BC in Campus Cyrunt, Egypt. Heber and his family left Crete and fought the ruling King of Scythia for a place of habitation and establishment of his colony. Heber ultimately prevailed against the King and continued there for four generations. Heber Scut was afterwards slain in battle by Noemus, the former king's son. The epithet "Scut" became known as "a Scot" or "a Scythian," and was applied to Heber. His son was Baouman.

King Baouman
(Twentieth Generation)

Baouman was King of Scythia and born in 2071 BC in Scythia. He died in Scythia. War and peace succeeded each other for a number of years upon which Baouman subsequently fell by the sword. His son was Ogaman.

King Ogaman
(Twenty-first Generation)

Ogaman was King of Scythia and was born in 2051 BC in Scythia. Using most of his father's fortune, Ogaman took command of the shattered fighting forces, and by courage and perseverance, became the next

King of Scythia. He also fell in battle after which his son Tait ascended the throne.

King Tait
(Twenty-second Generation)

Tait was King of Scythia and was born in 2026 BC in Scythia. He was slain and lost the throne in battle. His son was Agnon.

Agnon
(Twenty-third Generation)

Agnon was born in 2003 BC in Scythia and died in the Mediterranean Sea. This prince so inflamed the ruling class in battle that he was forced to prepare his ships and proceed to sea, leaving the area forever. Agnon and his followers wandered the coasts of the Mediterranean Sea for several years after which time he died. He had three sons, Ealloid, Lamhglass, and Lamhfionn.

Lamhfionn
(Twenty-fourth Generation)

Lamhfionn was born in 1980 BC in Scythia and died in Gothia, Africa. Upon his father's death, Lamhfionn and his colony periodically rested and refreshed themselves as they sojourned westward. Lamhfionn's spiritual advisor, Cachear, foretold there would be no end of their travels until they arrived and settled at the western island of Europe, today known as Ireland. Cachear prophesied that Ireland would become the place of destiny for their future, lasting settlement, and posterity. Lamhfionn died in the region of Gothia, today known as Libya, on the northern coast of Africa. His son was Heber Glunfionn.

King Heber Glunfionn
(Twenty-fifth Generation)

Heber Glunfionn was the first King of Gothia who was born in 1958 BC in Carthage, North Africa. His posterity would continue for another eight generations, during which time their lives were unremarkable and assumed to have been a period of relative peace and prosperity. His son was Agnan Fion.

King Agnan Fion
(Twenty-sixth Generation)

Agnon was the second King of Gothia who was born in 1938 BC in Gothia. Historians know very little about the history of Gothia (Libya) as there are few surviving written records. Libyan history is primarily known from archaeological evidence and sources written by their Egyptian neighbors, the ancient Greeks, Romans, Byzantines, and from Arabs of Medieval times. Agnon's son was Febric Glas.

King Febric Glas
(Twenty-seventh Generation)

Febric, the third King of Gothia, was born in 1920 BC in Gothia. With its bustling ports and growing sea trade, the climate in Gothia would have been dry and arid. In this ancient time, the Phoenicians would rule the ports and trade in the Mediterranean. His son was Nenuall.

King Nenuall
(Twenty-eighth Generation)

Nenuall, the fourth King of Gothia, born in 1899 BC in Gothia.

The exact boundaries of Ancient Gothia (Libya) are unknown. It was known at the time to be located somewhere west of Ancient Egypt. Generations later, the ancient Greeks considered Libya as one of the three known continents along with Asia and Europe. Nenuall fathered a son named Nuadhad.

King Nuadhad
(Twenty-ninth Generation)

Nuadhad was the fifth King of Gothia, born 1880 BC in Gothia. In the time of Nuadhad, his kingdom of Gothia (Libya) would have been the whole known African continent to the west of the Nile and extended south alongside of Egypt. Generations later, the Greek historian Herodotus described the inhabitants of Libya as two people, the Libyans in northern Africa and Ethiopians in the southern part of Africa. Nuadhad had a son named Alladh.

King Alladh
(Thirtieth Generation)

Alladh was the sixth King of Gothia, born in 1858 BC in Gothia. According to Herodotus, Libya (ancient Gothia) began where Ancient Egypt ended, and its territory extended to Cape Spartel, south of Tangier on the Atlantic coast. During his reign of peace, prosperity, and changing climate conditions, Alladh had a son named Arcadh.

King Arcadh
(Thirty-first Generation)

Arcadh was the seventh King of Gothia, born 1838 BC in Gothia. He married Lowra, who was born in 1835 BC. King Arcadh represented the seventh of eight unremarkable generations since the time of King Heber Glunfionn, one-hundred-twenty years earlier. It would be his grandson Brath who would lead the Gothian colony westward in search of their prophesied land of destiny. Arcadh and Lowra had a son named Deag.

King Deag
(Thirty-second Generation)

Deag, the eighth King of Gothia, was born in 1829 BC in Gothia. During his reign, the ancient Gothians in Libya were most likely nomads living off the land and raising goats, sheep, and other types of livestock. Libyan men are said to have had braided and beaded long hair and wore thin robes of animal skins. Women would have had decorated hair and similar robes as the men. Weapons would have included bows and arrows, hatchets, spears, and daggers made from rocks. This would have been the eighth and last generation that ruled in relative peace and prosperity. New battles would soon emerge on the horizon. King Deag had a son named Brath.

King Brath
(Thirty-third Generation)

Brath, the ninth King of Gothia, was born in 1815 BC in Gothia. Remembering the prediction foretold to his seventh great-grandfather Lamhfionn, and now being a ruler of a considerably larger colony in Gothia, Brath departed with a large fleet of ships to seek out the country (Ireland) destined for their final settlement. After some time sailing westward in the Mediterranean Sea, Brath and his colony landed upon the coast of Spain. They invaded the territory and established his colony in Galicia, located in the north of the country. Years later he died in Galicia, Spain, leaving behind a son named Breoghan.

King Breoghan
(Thirty-fourth Generation)

Breoghan, or Brigus, was the first King of the nations of Galicia, Andalusia, Murcia, Castile, and Portugal. He was born in 1799 BC in Gothia, Africa. Breoghan was a fierce warrior king and conquered the territories of Galicia, Andalusia, Murcia, Castile, and all of Portugal. The city of Brigansa or Braganza in northeast Portugal is named after him. He built Breoghan's Tower, also known as Brigantia. "Castile" was an independent Spanish kingdom in central Spain, on the central plateau of the Iberian Peninsula.

During his reign, Brigus sent a colony into Britain. They settled in a territory now known as the counties of York, Lancaster, Durham, Westmoreland, and Cumberland. Nearly 1,800 years later, the Brigantes would become known as a Celtic tribe who controlled the largest section of what would become Northern England in pre-Roman times. His Brigantian descendants were centered in what was later known as Yorkshire and whose posterity gave formidable oppositions to the first century AD Roman invasion of Britain. This King Breoghan died of unknown causes, if not from a fiercely lived life, in Galicia, Spain. His sons were Ithe and Bile.

King Bile MacGalcia
(Thirty-fifth Generation)

Bile was the second King of Galicia, Andulusia, Murcia, Castile, and Portugal. He was born in 1781 BC in Spain and he died in Spain. The life of Bile is sparsely known other than he became the king of those countries after his father's death. Upon his own death, his son, Galamh, also known as Galav or Milesius, succeed him and became the next great warrior king. From him the next one-hundred-nine generations would descend and influence the world, unlike any other bloodline in history.

After five-hundred years and twenty-two generations of migration throughout the Mediterranean region, we eagerly look towards the next age. Invasions of already-settled lands would continue and royal bloodlines would take on a more structured and sovereign existence. Our journey that began with Adam in the Garden of Eden, will next turn northward to the British Isles and more specifically, Éire, the Gaelic name for Ireland. Éire is a 27,000-square mile island nation in the North Atlantic Ocean, and a treacherous 540 nautical miles from Spain. This one family under God would continue to descend as a nomadic tribe that would invade an island nation, under the most uncertain and unexpected circumstances.

Antique map of Ireland by Thomas Jefferys (1772). This is the region in which the Irish Kings fought for provincial and national sovereignty for a period over more than a millennium.

Chapter 7

The Age of Irish Kings (1763 BC)

The next twenty-three generations extend over a course of more than one-thousand years, in what I am calling the Age of Irish Kings. The *Irish Chronicles* and Annalists provide records of a continuing succession of appointed monarchs rising to power by either bloodline succession or battles between descendants within and between one family. It is an amazing succession of regional lordship within what we know today as the Republic of Ireland and Northern Ireland.

The patriarch of The Age of Irish Kings is a historic warrior and general of armies in ancient Scythia and Egypt. Through his fighting power and leadership, he became the sovereign King of Galacia, an ancient region that today we know as the countries of Spain and Portugal. Much like the English settlers who colonized America after the original Native American settlers, this king and his descendants colonized Ireland after the original Irish settlers. Like the colonization of America, this king and his descendant engaged in an ancient civil war over a period of one-thousand years.

Like the first murder by Cain of Able in the Age of Creation, the patriarch's youngest son would kill one of his brothers, in order to reign supreme. As I researched and learned more about this time in history, the chronicles suggest it was like an ancient wild-wild west. With the scant information available, I found myself experiencing combined emotions of bewilderment, amazement, excitement, and profound gratitude for my own existence when researching and writing about this period.

The fighting, killing, treachery, and succession of generations that followed only served to underscore my belief that despite the sins of man, God's creation continued in its majesty. For it was during this time that the goodness of God continued as people became more civilized, cultures became more enlightened, and civilization expanded throughout Ireland and beyond.

The journey throughout this period is extraordinarily interesting. Monarchs like "Lord of Death," "The Prophet," and "The Big-Headed" bring a certain intrigue to this ancestral story. It's the connection between generations and continuity from Adam that continue to excite the probability of a humankind connection.

King Galamh Milesius
(Thirty-sixth Generation)

Galmah Milesius was third King of Galicia, Andulusia, Murcia, Castile, and Portugal. He was born in 1763 BC in the city of Brigantia, Galicia. He died in 1699 BC in the city of Braganza in the province of Iberia, Spain.

During his father's lifetime, Milesius went into Scythia, where he was kindly received by Reflor, the king of that country. On his arrival, Reflor gave Milesius his daughter Seang in marriage. Before Seang died and left Milesius a widower, he fathered two sons with her and they were named Arreagh Foevrach and Donn.

During his time in Scythia, Milesius was appointed General of Reflor's fighting forces. Milesius defeated his king's enemies and gained much love, fame, and fortune from all of the king's subjects. Over time, Reflor became jealous of Milesius and privately intended to banish him from Scythia. Upon learning of Reflor's intended admonishment, Milesius killed the king and left for Egypt with an armada of sixty ships.

Pharaoh Nectonibus learned of Milesius' arrival in Egypt and made plans to recognize his great valor and accomplishments in battle. The Pharaoh immediately made Milesius general of all his forces with a mission to invade the kingdom of Ethiopia. As in Scythia, Milesius was victorious and found great favor with Nectonibus, who gave him his daughter, Scota, in marriage. Milesius, Scota, and their family remained in Egypt for another eight years thereafter. Scota was born in 1765 BC in Egypt and died in 1699 BC in the village of Clahane, County Kerry, Ireland.

While Milesius was in Egypt, he employed the best and brightest of his colony to be instructed in the Egyptian trades, arts, and sciences so that they could transfer their knowledge back to his people in Spain. Upon his return to Spain, he was at once received by his people with great joy and renewed hope that he could counter the attacks from the natives and other nations that forced themselves into the country after his father's death.

Milesius immediately led his forces to reclaim their lands. After fighting and winning fifty-four battles, his forces completely routed, destroyed, and expatriated the rebellious natives and invading nations out of his country.

Sometime later, Milesius sent his uncle Ithe and Ithe's son Lughaidh to bring back an account of the western islands offshore from Spain which would later become known as Ireland. Ithe also brought along one-hundred-fifty valiant men for their journey to this largely unknown and potentially hostile land.

When Ithe arrived in Ireland, he was honorably received by the natives who were known as the tribe of Tuath-de-Danans. Ithe and his landing party were seen to be cultured and civilized people. The tribe found Ithe to be a man of great wisdom. Ithe urged the natives to co-exist with mutual love, peace, and forbearance. He praised the land of the Tuath-de-Danans to be a delightful, pleasant, and fruitful country. Ithe's civility was met with suspicious hostility by the natives who subsequently pursued Ithe with vigor and brutality on his return to Spain.

The Tuath-de-Danans fought and routed Ithe and overtook his men before his son Lughaidh could come to his rescue. Lughaidh found Ithe and returned to Spain with the dead and mangled body of his father, and thereupon exposed him in public view to excite his friends and relations to avenge his father's murder.

It should be noted that the original invaders and planters of Ireland who had killed Ithe, were originally Scythians of the line of Japheth that included the Tuatha-de-Danans. It is curious that Ithe and the Tuatha-dc-Danans misunderstood one another, since both spoke the same language, perhaps with some difference in accent. Nevertheless, it was likely less about language and more about greed, power, and frightful envy.

The exposing of the dead body of Ithe had the desired effect whereupon Milesius made great preparations to invade Ireland and avenge his uncle's death. For this Irish invasion, he left the care and charge of the expedition to his eight legitimate sons by his two wives.

Shortly after the death of Milesius, sons Heber, Heremon (Irwin), and Amergin, along with their five brothers and a well-equipped fleet, sailed into violent storms to the coasts of Ireland with an intent of invasion and settlement. The bloody battles resulted in overthrow and death of three Tuatha-de-Danans kings and queens and defeat of their armies. Heber, Heremon, and Amergin were the only brothers who survived the violent storms and raging battles with the Tuatha-de-Danans.

The history books of Ireland remark that another chief motive for Milesius and his colony to leave Spain and adventure into Ireland, was due to a great Spanish famine. The famine was partly due to an incursion of foreigners, but mainly from a strange, prolonged drought which lasted twenty-six years during which no rain fell in that country. This invasion, conquest or plantation of Ireland by the Milesian or Scottish Nation, took place during the seventeenth year of the drought in 1700 BC.

Heremon was the youngest of the three sons who survived their invasion of Ireland, and from him descended one-hundred-fourteen sole Monarchs of Ireland including the provincial Kings and Hermonian gentry of the regions of Clannaboy, Tirowen, and Tirconnel; the kingdoms of Leinster, Connaught, Orgiall, and Meath; the Kings of Dál Riata; all the Kings of Scotland from Fergus Mór MacEarea, down to the Stuarts; and the Kings and Queens of England from Henry the Second down to the present time.

King Heremon Eochaidh
(Thirty-seventh Generation)

Heremon and his younger brother Heber commanded joint sovereignty for one year before Heber was slain by Heremon due to a quarrel that was preceded by the pride and ambition of Heber's wife. Heremon subsequently slayed his other brother Amergin. As such, Heremon became the second High King of Ireland, born in 1750 BC in Braganza, Iberia, Spain.

Consequently, Heremon became the sole monarch of Ireland, after which he made new divisions within the country to be ruled by his friends and comrades in arms. The province of Munster was ruled by his brother Heber's four sons, Er, Orba, Feron, and Fergina. The northern part of Ireland, today known as Ulster, was ruled by Heber Donn, son of one of his deceased brothers lost in battle. The eastern part (Leinster) and western part (Connaught) of Ireland were ruled by Heremon's commanders. Part of Munster was ruled by Lughaidh, the son of Ithe, the first Milesian family of Ireland.

Heremon died in 1683 BC in Ross, Ireland. He married Teia Ingen Lugdach, daughter of Lughaidh Mac Ith and Fial Nic Miled. She was born in 1736 BC. The Royal Seat of Tara was erected by Teia, for the habitation and burial place of her children. Their son was Irial Faidh.

King Irial Faidh "The Prophet"
(Thirty-eighth Generation)

Irial Faidh was the tenth High King of Ireland. He was born in 1724 BC in Braganza, Spain. He was nicknamed "The Prophet" from being carefully bred and influenced in the arts by the Druids. A Druid was a member of the educated, professional class among the Celtic people including lawspeakers, poets, doctors, and other learned professions including religious leaders. During his reign of ten years, Irial cleared woods from a good part of the country resulting in the creation of sixty-one plains, Royal forts, and the three rivers called the three fins, which broke out in the north of Ireland. He died a natural death in 1670 BC in the town of Magh Muaagh, County Galway in the Province of Connaught, Ireland. His son was Eithrial Faidh.

King Eithrial Faidh
(Thirty-ninth Generation)

Eithrial Faidh was the eleventh High King of Ireland, born in 1700 BC at Magh Muaagh, Ireland. During his sovereignty of twenty years, Eithrial imitated his father by cutting down an abundance of woods to make the land more habitable. He also cleared seven great plains where battles were fought from time to time. Though a lover of peace and addicted to the improvement of land, Eithrial was killed at the battle of Soirrean, in Leinster, in 1650 BC. Eithrial died at the hands of his cousin, Conmaol (twelfth High King of Ireland), son of Heber from the town of Siorrean in the Province of Leinster. Eithrial had a son whose name was Follach.

Follach
(Fortieth Generation)

Follach, Prince of Ireland, was born in 1663 BC in County Meath, Ireland. He died in 1616 BC at Meath, Ireland. Follach was prevented from succeeding his father as monarch due to his death at the hands of his uncle Conmaol. Follach's son was Tighernmhas.

King Tighernmhas "Lord of Death"
(Forty-first Generation)

Tighernmhas, the thirteenth High King of Ireland, was born about 1640 BC in Meath, Ireland. He reigned for fifty years and fought twenty-seven battles during his monarchy. Historians observed that after discovering gold and silver mines in the country, King Tighernmhas was the first to have introduced idolatry amongst the natives. During his prolific reign, nine lakes broke out of the earth. He fought twenty-seven battles against the progeny of Heber, and their followers and affiliates. He died suddenly on November 1, 1543 BC at Magh Sleaght (or Field of Adoration), in the county of Leitrim, Ireland. He had married Sinusa Maceochaidh I, Princess and Queen of Ireland. Sinusa was born before 1569 BC in Meath, Ireland. She died in Meath, Ireland. Their son was Enbotha.

Enbotha
(Forty-second Generation)

Enbotha was Prince of Ireland. He was born about 1556 BC and died about 1513 BC in Meath, Ireland. The Kingdom of Ireland was divided into two parts from Drogheda to Limerick during his lifetime. His son was Simorgoill.

Simorgoill
(Forty-third Generation)

Simorgoill was born about 1523 BC in Meath, Ireland. He died about 1480 BC at Tara Castle in Meath, Ireland. Tara Castle, located in the Hill of Tara, was once the ancient seat of power in Ireland. The Hill of Tara is located near the River Boyne and today is an archaeological complex located in Meath, Ireland. The Picts were subjugated by the Irish monarchy during his lifetime. Simorgoill's son was Fiacha Labhrainne.

King Fiacha Labhrainne
(Forty-fourth Generation)

Fiacha Labhrainne was the eighteenth High King of Ireland. In ancient times, the name Fiacha is known as "a hunter" and was a frequent name of kings and chiefs. He was born about 1482 BC at Tara Castle in Meath, Ireland. All the inhabitants of Scotland were subjected to the Irish monarchy during his rule. During his twenty-four-year reign, he fought in three battles against the Heberians and died in 1448 BC when he was killed in the Battle of Bealgadain at Kilbreedy Major Parish, Ireland. He married Morolach, Queen of Ireland at Tara Castle in Meath, Ireland. She was born before 1440 BC at Tara Castle in Meath, Ireland. She died at Tara Castle in Meath, Ireland. Their son was Aengus Olmuchadha.

King Aengus Olmuchadha "The Big Headed One"
(Forty-fifth Generation)

Aengus Olmuchadha was the twentieth High King of Ireland. He was born about 1453 BC at Tara Castle in Meath, Ireland. During the tenth year of his eighteen-year reign, he is believed to be the first King mentioned to have gone on an expedition against the Picts, a tribal coalition of people who lived in eastern and northern Scotland. The Picts were the original pre-Roman inhabitants and became known as Picts because their language was pictorial. He died in 1409 BC when he was slain in the Battle of Carman (Wexford) by Enna (Twenty-first High King of Ireland). His son was Maen.

Maen
(Forty-sixth Generation)

Maen was born in 1435 BC and died in 1350 BC at Tara Castle in Meath, Ireland. He married Hvarfiad of Ireland. She was born in 1402 BC at Tara Castle in Meath, Ireland. King Ennius reigned during the time of Maen and was the first Monarch mentioned that got silver shields wrought for the grandees of the Kingdom, which earned him much affection of the Nobility throughout the country. Maen and Hvarfiad had a son whose name was Rothechtaid.

King Rothechtaid
(Forty-seventh Generation)

Rothechtaid was the twenty-second High King of Ireland. He was born in 1415 BC at Tara Castle in Meath, Ireland. He died in 1375 BC; slain by Cruachain in the Battle of Rath Croghan (Rathcroghan), County Roscommon, Connaught Province, Ireland. His son was Deman.

Deman
(Forty-eighth Generation)

Deman was born in 1382 BC at Tara Castle in Meath, Ireland. In his days, King Munemon made a famous law that the nobility should wear a chain of gold around their necks. Henceforth, no man, unless belonging to the truly ancient and Noble Order of Knighthood of Milesians, was capable of being elected King without first being a Knight of the Chain. Denman died in 1322 BC in Roscommon, Ireland. His son was Dian Dain.

Dian Dain
(Forty-ninth Generation)

Dian Dain was born about 1326 BC at Tara Castle in Meath, Ireland and died about 1242 BC. His son was Sirna Saoghalach.

King Sirna Saoghalach "The Long Lived"
(Fiftieth Generation)

Sirna Saoghalach was the thirty-fourth High King of Ireland. He was born in 1243 BC at Tara Castle in Meath, Ireland and died in 1130 BC in Bayern, Germany, having traveled to this distant land for unknown reasons. His son was Olioll Olchain.

Olioll Olchain
(Fifty-first Generation)

Olioll Olchain was born 1183 BC and died 1090 BC at Tara Castle in Meath, Ireland. His son was Giallchaidh.

King Giallchaidh
(Fifty-second Generation)

Giallchaidh was the thirty-seventh High King of Ireland who was born about 1100 BC at Tara Castle in Meath, Ireland. He died in 1013 BC, killed by his cousin, Art Imleach (thirty-eighth High King of Ireland) at the town of Moighe Muadh in Connaught, Ireland. His son was Nuadhat Finnfail.

King Nuadhat Finnfail
(Fifty-third Generation)

Nuadhat Finnfail was the thirty-ninth High King of Ireland and reigned for forty years. He was born in 1021 BC at Tara Castle in Meath, Ireland and died in 962 BC in Meath, where he was slain by his cousin, Breasrioghacta, his successor as fortieth High King of Ireland. His son was Aedhan Glas.

Aedhan Glas
(Fifty-fourth Generation)

Aedhan Glas was born in 981 BC and died 930 BC at Tara Castle in Meath, Ireland. During his lifetime, the Irish coast was overrun by pirates and a dreadful plague killed most of the inhabitants along the shoreline. His son was Simeon Breac.

King Simeon Breac
(Fifty-fifth Generation)

Simeon Breac was the forty-fourth High King of Ireland. He was born about 932 BC at Tara Castle in Meath, Ireland and died in 903 BC.

Simeon was brutally dismembered by order of Duach Fionn, the son of the forty-third King Sedna Innarraigh. The cruel mutilation of Simeon Breach by Duach Fionn was in revenge of his father's (Sedna Innarraigh) murder by Simeon. His son was Muireadhach Bolgrach.

King Muireadhach Bolgrach
(Fifty-sixth Generation)

Muireadhach Bolgrach was the forty-sixth High King of Ireland. Muireadhach is a name equivalent to that of "admiral," derived from *muir*, "the sea," and *eachach*, "a protector." The anglicized names for Muireadhach are Maurice and Murray. He was born in 912 BC at Tara Castle in Meath, Ireland. He died in 892 BC. His two sons were Duach Teamhrach and Fiacha Tolgrach.

King Fiacha Tolgrach
(Fifty-seventh Generation)

Fiacha Tolgrach was the fifty-fifth High King of Ireland. He was born in 850 BC at Tara Castle in Meath, Ireland. He died in 795 BC, when he was killed by his cousin, Oilioll Finn (successor as fifty-sixth High King of Ireland) in a sword fight at Tara Hill. His brother Duach had two sons, Eochaidh Framhuine and Conang Beag-eaglach, who became the fifty-first and fifty-third Monarchs of Ireland. His son was Duach Ladhgrach.

King Duach Ladhgrach
(Fifty-eighth Generation)

Duach Ladhgrach was the fifty-ninth High King of Ireland and reigned for ten years. He was born in 829 BC at Tara Castle in Meath,

Ireland. He died in 737 BC when he was slain by Lughaidh Laighdhea (successor as sixtieth High King of Ireland) at Tara Hill. His son was Eochaidh Buadhach.

The next age ushers in a millennium of exciting developments. While monarchs continue to battle for sovereign rule, the culture becomes more civilized and generally peaceful. A legendary religious artifact arrives in the kingdom with an effect of aligning belief in God's sovereignty by both rulers and the people. A warrior-king is born at the end of this age and he would have a significant impact on the demise of Mediterranean invaders and sunset of an ancient civilization. We look forward to the next generations.

An accurate map of the Holy Land divided into the twelve tribes of Israel accommodated to sacred history and describing the travels of Jesus Christ by Emmanuel Bowen (1752). Courtesy Library of Congress Geography and Maps Division. This is the ancient region from which the Covenant Stone, or Stone of Destiny is believed to have originated.

Chapter 8

The Age of Covenant Kings (751 BC)

T he next thirty-one generations extend over a course of more than one-thousand years, in what I am calling the Age of Covenant Kings. This period in history is marked by several contradictions with respect to timelines, inter-race marriage, and the birth of the King of kings, Jesus Christ. Jesus Christ and His ancestry are not the primary consideration of *The Adam Connection*, however, Christians believe that Jesus Christ is the Son of God. He is one of the Holy Trinity (the Father, the Son, and the Holy Spirit existing as one God), which makes Him God. So, in that context, I believe remarks about Jesus and His reign during the Covenant Irish Kings is both pragmatic and purposeful.

There seem to be no accounts in the Irish Chronicles about a princess daughter of the last king of Judah who fled Israel from Babylonian persecution. The princess is said to have been accompanied on her journey to Ireland by the prophet Jeremiah, and what was known at the time as the "Stone of the Covenant." This religious artifact became known by other names over time, and would accompany the coronations of some of the most influential British monarchs in history to present day. While this artifact is real, the legendary Jewish princess and her story is disputed, but possible.

It was during this period that the annalists provided scant details about names, dates, people, and noteworthy events. Having said that,

I note that these generations were descendants of Scythian ancestors and certain references are provided for context. At the turn of the second millennium, we learn about kings who fought dozens of battles to restore their royal bloodline, and other monarchs who fought hundreds of battles to consolidate power in their kingdom. We learn about Covenant Irish Kings who ruled with wisdom and the rule of law, and others who applied the law in a moral and ethical manner.

We increasingly witness periods of peace and security. Yes, there continues to be battles for territory and power, but one has the sense that rulers in this age were becoming more influenced by the needs of their people. New characters with nicknames like "The Beautiful," "Hospitable," and "Law Giver" emerge to provide a sense of hope for the future. In these ancient times, a covenant was often defined as an agreement or relationship between God and His people. With the Stone of Destiny, birth of Jesus Christ, and royal bloodlines, we see that generational connections continue for this ancestral family, if not for all of humankind.

Eochaidh Buadhach "The Conqueror" (Fifty-ninth Generation)

Eochaidh Buadhach was born in 751 BC in Tara Castle. He died in 683 BC. During his reign, the plague visited his kingdom on two occasions. Legend says he married Tamara Tea Tephi ben Zedekiah. While the dates of her birth and death do not coincide with his life, the sheer volume of accounts of their marriage gives rise to their possible union. Tamara was also known as Daughter of God's House, Queen of Ireland, Princess of Judah, and of the House of David.

Her father, Zedekiah, was the last King of Judah. Because of his marriage to Tamara Tea Tephi's, Eochaidh Buadhach's family would have descended from Abraham, Isaac, Jacob, Judah, as well as the first three Kings of Israel Saul, David, and Solomon.

Kings of Israel and Judah

Saul	1050-1010 BC
David	1010- 970 BC
Solomon	970- 930 BC

Kings of Judah

Rehoboam	931–913 BC
Abijah	913–911 BC
Asa	911–870 BC
Jehoshaphat	870–848 BC
Jehoram	848–841 BC
Ahaziah	841 BC
Athaliah	841-835 BC
Joash	835-796 BC
Amaziah	796-767 BC
Uzziah	767-740 BC
Jotham	740-732 BC
Ahaz	732-716 BC
Hezekiah	716-687 BC
Manasseh	687-642 BC
Amon	642-640 BC
Josiah	640-608 BC
Jehoahaz	608 BC
Jehoiakim	608-597 BC
Jehoiachin	597 BC
Zedekiah	597-586 BC

The Kings of Judah were monarchs who ruled over the ancient Kingdom of Judah. After the death of Saul, the Tribe of Judah elevated David to rule over the kingdoms of Israel and Judah. After seven years, David became king of a reunited Kingdom of Israel.

Legend says the Prophet Jeremiah rescued the Royal Blood Line of David by fleeing to Ireland with Tamara to avoid persecution and perhaps death at the hands of the Babylonian King Nebuchadnezzar, whose army conquered Judah. Tamara fled with the Riblah, Israel, with the anointed "Stone of the Covenant," which was also known as: Jacob's Pillow, Stone of Scone, and Lia Fail (Stone of Destiny).

Historically, this anointed artifact was kept at Scone Abbey in Scone, near Perth, Scotland. The stone is 26 inches by 16.75 inches by 10.5 inches, and weighs approximately 336 pounds. An incised cross is on one surface. The Stone of Destiny has since been put under the coronation chair of the Kings and Queens of Scotland, Ireland, and England. It was last used in 1953, for the coronation of Elizabeth II of the United Kingdom. The Stone of Destiny rests under the coronation chair in Westminster Abbey in London. A sign beside this ancient artifact reads, "Jacob's pillar-stone" (Genesis 28:18 NIV).

The royal marriage between Eochaidh and the Jewish Princess Tamara produced a son named Ugaine.

King Ugaine Mor "The Great" (Sixtieth Generation)

Ugaine was the sixty-sixth High King of Ireland and considered one of the most famous Pagan Monarchs. He was born in 691 BC at Tara Castle in Meath, Ireland, and died in 593 BC. Ugaine was called Mor (the great) because of his sovereignty over all the islands of Western Europe. It would have been around 612 BC that Ugaine's

Scythian ancestors joined the Babylonians and Persians to destroy the Assyrian Empire.

Ugaine was much celebrated for his successful expeditions throughout the Mediterranean and his marriage to Caesair Cruthach, daughter of the King of the Gauls, Princess of France, Queen of Ireland. She was born in 634 BC in France. Caesair was so striking in her physical appearance that she was nicknamed "The Beautiful" and with Ugaine they had twenty-two sons and three daughters. For their children's inheritance, Ugaine divided Ireland into twenty-five sections in order to impose taxes and other heavy duties. Ugaine was slain by Badhbhchadh for rights to the Irish throne and Caesair died at Tara Castle in Meath, Ireland. One of their sons was Cobhthach Cael Breagh.

King Cobhthach Cael Breagh "The Meagre"
(Sixty-first Generation)

Cobhthach Cael Breagh was sixty-ninth High King of Ireland and reigned for thirty years. He was born in 621 BC at Tara Castle in Meath, Ireland, and died in 541 BC. He ascended the throne after killing his brother from ruling his portion of the country called Bregaive, which in Latin is Bregia, meaning emotional and needing to be loved. His nephew, Maison, killed King Cobhthach at Tara Castle in Meath, Ireland. The son of Cobhthach Cael Breagh was Melghe Molbhtach.

King Melghe Molbhtach "The Praiseworthy"
(Sixty-second Generation)

Melghe Molbhtach was the seventy-first High King of Ireland, and reigned for twelve years. He was born in 558 BC at Tara Castle in Meath, Ireland. Melghe was killed by the sword of Modhchorbv, son of Cobhthach in 505 BC at County Clare in the province of Leinster, Ireland. Melghe was an excellent Prince which got him the nickname of Molfach, which signified a man worthy to be praised. Melghe's son was Irereo Fathach.

King Irereo Fathach "The Wise"
(Sixty-third Generation)

Irereo Fathach was the seventy-fourth High King of Ireland and reigned for six years. Back in Persia, Irereo's Scythian ancestors successfully defended themselves against the powerful Persian ruler, Darius. Irereo succeeded to the throne after the death of his cousin, Aeneas, who was nicknamed "The Doctor" for his ability in learning. Irereo Fathach was born in 530 BC at Tara Castle in Meath, Ireland, and died in battle in 473 BC in County Ulster, Tyrone Province, Ireland. He had four sons Irereo, Doel, Darius, and Connla.

King Connla Caemh "The Beautiful"
(Sixty-fourth Generation)

Connla was the seventy-sixth High King of Ireland. He was born about 491 BC and died in 442 BC at Tara Castle in Meath, Ireland. He married Sabhdh MacEochaidh at Tara Castle. She was born before 437 BC and died at Tara Castle in Meath, Ireland. Their son was Oilioll.

King Oilioll Caisfhiaclach "Crooked Teeth"
(Sixty-fifth Generation)

Oilioll Caisfhiaclach, the seventy-seventh High King of Ireland, reigned over the Kingdom for twenty-five years. He was born in 460 BC at Tara Castle in Meath, Ireland. He had better luck then some other Princes as he immediately succeeded his father. He had a deformed, uneven set of teeth, hence, his nickname. Adamair (Seventy-seventh King), son of Fearcorb, killed him by the sword in 417 BC. Oilioll's son was Eochaidh Ailtleathan.

King Eochaidh Ailtleathan "Long Hair"
(Sixty-sixth Generation)

Eochaidh Ailtleathan was the seventy-ninth High King of Ireland who reigned for seven years. He was born in 435 BC at Tara Castle in Meath, Ireland. He was known for his big frame and thick, burly hair. He married Agnus who died in Ireland. He fell in battle in 395 BC at Tara Hill. Their son was Aengus Tuirmheach-Teamhrach.

King Aengus Tuirmheach-Teamhrach "Bashful"
(Sixty-seventh Generation)

Aengus Tuirmheach-Teamhrach, the eighty-first High King of Ireland, reigned for sixty years. He was born about 400 BC at Tara Castle in Meath, Ireland. He was the first in Ireland who raised bee-hives in meadows and mossy grounds as opposed to building the hives in hollows of trees. He died in 325 BC at Tara Castle. He married Ingen Aengus, Queen of Ireland. She was born before 383 BC in Meath, Ireland. She died at Tara Castle. Aengus and Ingen had two sons, Enna and Fiacha, both of whom are celebrated in history as ancestors of several tribes and noble families. Since ancient manuscripts require thoughtful investigation, it is not completely surprising that medieval scholars disagree on the next twenty-seven generations that converge again in some seven-hundred years. Aengus and wife Ingen had a son, Enna Aighneach.

King Enna Aighneach "The Hospitable"
(Sixty-eighth Generation)

Enna Aighneach was the eighty-fourth High King of Ireland. He was born 370 BC at Tara Castle in Meath, Ireland. He died in 292 BC at Tara Castle in Meath, Ireland, when he was killed in his bed at the hands of Criomthan Cosgrach (successor as the eighty-fifth High King of Ireland). Enna's son was Labraidh Lorc.

Labraidh Lorc
(Sixty-ninth Generation)

Labraidh Lorc was born about 356 BC and died about 280 BC in Tara Castle. He married Sabilla in Tara Hill. She was born before 353 BC in Meath, Ireland, and died at Tara Castle in Meath, Ireland. Their son was Blathacht.

Blathacht
(Seventieth Generation)

Blathacht was born about 340 BC and died about 280 BC at Tara Castle in Meath, Ireland. He married Magach, Princess of Ireland, who was born before 333 BC in Meath, Ireland. She died in Tara. Their son was Essamain Emna.

Essamain Emna
(Seventy-first Generation)

Essamain Emna was born about 320 BC and died about 260 BC in Tara, Ireland. He married Magach (Margaret) of Ireland. She was born in 333 BC and died in Meath, Ireland. Their son was Roignein Ruadh.

Roignein Ruadh "The Red"
(Seventy-second Generation)

Roignein Ruadh was born about 300 BC and died about 240 BC in Tara, Ireland. He married Benia Ingen Criomthan Niadh Nar of Ireland. She was born and died in Dublin, Leinster Province, Ireland. Their son was Finnlogha.

Finnlogha "Fair Hero"
(Seventy-third Generation)

Finnlogha was born about 270 BC and died in 210 BC at Tara Castle in Meath, Ireland. This is one of the earliest known spellings of the surname "Finley." His son was Fionn O'Henna.

Fionn O'Henna
(Seventy-fourth Generation)

Fionn O'Henna was born about 212 BC and died about 178 BC at Tara Castle in Meath, Ireland. The name Fionn means "fair haired" and was a common name of many kings and chiefs. He married Benta, daughter of Creobthan. She was born about 182 BC and died in Leinster, Ireland. Their son was Eochaidh Feidhlioch.

King Eochaidh Feidhlioch "Melancholy"
(Seventy-fifth Generation)

Eochaidh Feidhlioch was the ninety-third High King of Ireland. He was born about 192 BC and died in 130 BC in Tara Castle. Eochaidh caused the twenty-five-part division of the Irish kingdom to cease and desist. In its place was the return of the ancient division into provinces of Munster, Leinster, Conacht, and Ulster. After this division of the Irish kingdom, Eochaidh constructed a new Royal Palace in Conacht. He married Cloth Fionn, daughter of Eochaidh Uchleathan, who was born and died in Ireland. Their son was Breas Nar Lotha.

King Breas Nar Lotha
(Seventy-sixth Generation)

Breas Nar Lotha was King of Leinster. He was born in 80 BC in Leinster, Ireland, and died in 45 BC in Tara, Ireland. It is during his reign that the Irish first began to dig underground graves for the dead and departed. Previously, dead bodies were laid on the ground covered by stones. Breas Nar Lotha married Clothra Verch Eochaid. She was born 80 BC and died in Tara, Ireland. Their son was Lugaidh Sriabhn Dearg.

King Lugaidh Sriabhn Dearg
(Seventy-seventh Generation)

Lugaidh Sriabhn Dearg was the ninety-eighth High King of Ireland. He was born in 45 BC in Dublin, Ireland, and died in 8 BC. During his reign, Lugaidh Sriabhn Dearg entered an alliance with the King of Denmark, and married Dearborguill, Princess of Denmark, in Dublin. She was born in 34 BC in Denmark. Dearborguill died in 9 BC at Tara Castle in Meath, Ireland. Their son was Crimthann Naidh Nar.

King Crimthann Naidh Nar "The Heroic"
(Seventy-eighth Generation)

Crimthann Naidh Nar was the one-hundredth High King of Ireland. He was born about 27 BC and died in 9 BC, after falling from a horse at the Fortress Dun Crimthann, in the town of Bin Edar on the Hill of Howth in Ireland. His death was preceded by successful expeditions and battles against the Romans in Britain, from which he brought back to Ireland many spoils including swords, shields, precious metal, gem laden ornaments, and other precious articles. He was first married to Nar-That-Chaoch, daughter of Laoch, who lived in the land of Picts in Scotland. His second marriage was to Baine, Princess of Ireland in Dublin. She was born in the Kingdom of Alba (Scotland). She died in Dublin, Ireland. Their son was Feredach Fionn Feachtnach.

King Feredach Fionn Feachtnach "The True and Sincere" (Seventy-ninth Generation)

Feredach Fionn Feachtnach was the one-hundred-second High King of Ireland. He was born about 9 BC in Dublin and died AD 36 at Tara Castle in Meath, Ireland. During his reign lived a man named Moran, a celebrated Chief Justice of the Kingdom of whom possessed a legendary "collar" that tested and proclaimed the accuracy of his judicial decisions. While the legend is documented, it was perhaps more symbolic of his fairness and justice. He married Chabob Mar Fath, who was born before 8 BC in Meath, Ireland. She died at Tara Castle in Meath, Ireland. Their son was Fiachadh Fionohudh.

King Fiachadh Fionohudh (Eightieth Generation)

Fiachadh Fionohudh was the one-hundred-fourth High King of Ireland. He was born about AD 10 at Tara Castle in Meath, Ireland, and died in AD 57 in the slaughter of Magh Bolg (Moybolgue Parish), Town of Cavan, Ulster County, Ireland. He married Either Nar, Princess of Alba. Fiachadh and Either had a son whose name was Tuathal Teachtmar.

Fiachadh would have been a contemporary of Jesus Christ. Most biblical scholars agree that Jesus was a Jewish teacher from Galilee, in the region of north Israel, who performed many miracles of healing and deliverance from pain and suffering. He called twelve Jewish men to be His disciples so that they would follow Him as Jesus prepared them to carry on His ministry.

Jesus Christ was crucified in Jerusalem by order of Pontius Pilate, the Roman governor, for claiming to be the King of the Jews. He resurrected three days after His death and then, according to scripture, ascended into heaven. Over time, followers of Jesus Christ became known as Christians. Among Christians, the traditional date for Jesus' death is believed to be AD 33. Christians believe Jesus' life and death provided the atoning sacrifice for the sins of the world that originated with Adam's original sin that separated man from God. It was through Jesus Christ's sacrifice on the cross that man was reconciled back to God and receive eternal salvation. Jesus Christ is considered the most influential person in the history of the world.

King Tuathal Teachtmar
(Eighty-first Generation)

Tuathal Teachtmar was the one-hundred-sixth High King of Ireland. The name Tuathal means one possessing large lands and territory. He was born in AD 56 in Tara, Ireland, and died in AD 106 when was slain by his successor, Mal of Ulster, in the town of Ceannaguha, near Tara. When Tuathal was a young man, his grandfather, the King of Alba, helped him establish provincial power within his family to overcome his enemies. There were twenty-five battles in Ulster, twenty-five in Leinster, as many in Connaught, and thirty-five in Munster. Having restored the true royal blood and their heirs to the respective provincial kingdoms, he extracted a tract of land from each province to create a new province named Midhe or "Meath." Meath then became the central place or capital, from which forty Monarchs over six-hundred years would reign.

Some noteworthy accomplishments by Tuathal included the building of the Royal Palace at Tailtean and resumption of Fairs on La Lughnasa (Lewy's Day), to which all the youth of both sexes of suitable age came to become married.

Tuathal married Baine Ingen Balbh, the daughter of Sgaile Balbh, the King of England. She was born in AD 75 in Alba and died in AD 145 at the town of Cnoc Baine located in the over-kingdom of Oirghialla (tribal confederation) in Ireland. Their son was Feidimidh Rectmar.

King Feidimidh Rectmar "The Law Giver"
(Eighty-second Generation)

Feidimidh Rectmar was the one-hundred-eighth High King of Ireland who reigned for nine years. He was born in AD 97 in Leinster, Ireland, and died of thirst while asleep in AD 119 in Tara, Ireland. He was so called the "Law Giver." He created excellent laws which preserved the people in peace, quiet, abundance, and security. He married Una Ughna, daughter of the King of Denmark. She was born AD 91 in Denmark and died in AD 119 in Ireland. Their son was the legendary Conn Ceadcathach

Conn Ceadcathach
(Eighty-third Generation)

Conn Ceadcathach was the one-hundred-tenth High King of Ireland and reigned for thirty-five years. The anglicized name for Conn is Constantine. The etymology of Conn is derived from conn, wisdom or con, a swift-footed warrior. He was born in AD 113 in Tara, Ireland and died in AD 157 at Tara Castle on the throne of the one-hundred-ninth High King, Tuath Amrois. He was barbarously slain by Tiobraidhe Tireach, grandson of Rochruidhe, King of Ulster. This murder was committed in Tara when fifty men, disguised as women, cornered Conn alone and unattended. His legendary encounters included sixty battles against Cahir Mór, King of Leinster; one hundred battles against the Ulsterians; and one hundred more in battles against Owen Mór, King of Munster. He married Eithue of Ireland, who was born in Leinster and died in AD 194 in County Galway, Connaught, Ireland. Their three daughters were Sadhbh, Maoin, and Sarah. Their son was named Art Eaufhear.

King Art Eaufhear
(Eighty-fourth Generation)

Art was the one-hundred-twelfth High King of Ireland. He was born in AD 150 in Ireland and died in AD 195 in the Battle of MagMucroimbe. He married Eachtach Nmn Art. She was born and died in Ireland. Their son was Cormac Ulfada.

King Cormac Ulfada "Long Beard"
(Eighty-fifth Generation)

Cormac Ulfada was the one-hundred-fifteenth High King of Ireland and reigned for forty years. The name Cormac signifies "the son of the chariot." He was born in AD 195 and died in AD 266 in the parish of Cleitoch on the River Boyne in Ireland. He was famous for his wise and fair decisions. In the Annals Clonmacnoise, a monastery in County Ofaly, Cormac was described as a wise and learned man who was not given to be causelessly bloody as were many of his ancestors. He was said to be eloquent, of action and valor, of royal sway, of domination, of emulation, of ethics, and vigorous.

He made Ireland a land of promise, free of theft, rape, and violence. He fought many battles, subduing the provinces of Ulaid (Ulster) and Connacht, and leading a lengthy campaign against the province of Munster. In the fourteenth year of his reign, he is said to have sailed to Britain and made conquests there. In his fifteenth year, thirty maidens were slaughtered in Tara by Dúnlaing, king of Leinster, for which Cormac had twelve Leinster princes put to death. He is said to have been temporarily deposed twice by the Ulaid people and was missing for four months. He is also said to have compiled the Psalter of Tara, a book containing the chronicles of Irish history, the laws concerning the rents and dues kings were to receive from their subjects, and records of the boundaries of Ireland.[43],[44] He married Eithne Ollamda, daughter of Dúnlaing, King of Leinster. She was born AD 185 in Dublin, Ireland, and died in Somme, France, where he may have been traveling to fight Roman invaders impinging their influence upon the British Isles. Cormac and Eithme had ten daughters and three sons, including Cairbre Liffeachaire.

King Cairbre Liffeachaire
(Eighty-sixth Generation)

Cairbre Liffeachaire was the one-hundred-fifteenth High King of Ireland. His reign was from AD 267–284. After Cairbre had been seventeen years in the sovereignty of Ireland, he fell in the battle of Gabhra Aichle, by the hand of Semeon, son of Cearb, one of the clan Fotharta

---

[43] Standish Hayes O'Grady, *The Panegyric of Cormac mac Airt*, (Reprint: C. Lemma Publishing Corporation).

[44] www.maryjones.us/ctexts/panegriccormac

Fearcorb. He married Aine (Hannah) Nichfinn Onuadu and one of their sons was Fiacha Sraibhtine.

King Fiacha Sraibhtine
(Eighty-seventh Generation)

Fiacha Sraibhtine was the one-hundred-twentieth High King of Ireland. He was born in AD 235 in the town of Dunsrabhteine in Connaught, Ireland. He died in 285 in the town of Dubhcomar, County Meath. He married Aiofe Dau Coel, daughter of the King of Gall. Their son was Tireach Murdeach.

King Murdeach Tireach
(Eighty-eighth Generation)

Murdeach Tireach was the one-hundred-twenty-second High King of Ireland. He was born in 273 in Tara, Ireland, and died in AD 326. He married Murion Cinneal Eoqin, daughter of Fiachadh, King of Ulster. She was born in AD 275 in Ulster, Ireland. She died in Great Britain. Muiredach was overthrown and killed by Cáelbad son of Cronn Bradruí, an Ulster king, but Cálbad only ruled one year before their son Eochaid killed him and took the throne.

King Eochaidh Muigh Meadhoin
(Eighty-ninth Generation)

Eochaidh Muigh Meadhoin was one-hundred-twenty-fourth High King of Ireland. The name Eochaidh signifies "a knight or horseman." He was born in AD 287 in Alba (Scotland) and died from poisoning at the hands of his first wife, in AD 357 in Tara, Ireland. After ruling for eight years, he was succeeded by Crimthann mac Fidaig, King of

Munster. By his first wife, Mong Fionn, he had four sons named Brion, Fiachra, Olioll III, and Fergus IV. His second wife, Inne Cairrion Chasdubh, was daughter of the King of the West Saxons. She was born in Lutherstadt Wittenberg, a town in Saxony, Germany. She died in Somme, France. Their son was Niall.

The upcoming century introduces one of the greatest warriors in *The Adam Connection*. He will become well-known for strategic warfare that influenced the transition from late middle ages to medieval times. Controversial bloodlines emerge in this next age, as do historical battles of which legends are made. Religious missionaries appear during this next period and they begin the process of converting the country to Christianity. Because of the many conflicts and contradictions, this next age can be both hard to believe and convincing.

Antique Map of the British Isles, engraved by Borde (circa 1760). This is the region from which an Irish King drove the Romans out of Great Britain.

Chapter 9

The Age of Roman
Re-conquest (AD 311)

—————————————◆—————————————

T he next four generations extend over a period of one-hundred-
fifty years, in what is called The Age of Roman Re-conquest.
This period is dominated by a remarkable Irish warrior-king who
fought back the occupation of Britain by the Romans at the twilight
of Rome's ancient empire. The invasion of Britain by Rome began in
the early first century AD, and occupied most of the country up to the
border of modern day Scotland. It is within this context that *The Adam
Connection* continues.

Considered one of the greatest warriors of medieval Ireland, the
warrior-king fought courageously to expel the Roman occupiers in
Britannia. His was the first generation that followed an ancient native
Irish law that was named after wandering lawyers called the "Brehons."
Brehon law described the ancient life of Ireland characterized by mud
huts, circular shaped settlements, and exchange of agricultural goods
as a form of barter. By the seventeenth century that would follow,
Brehon law was eclipsed by English law which patterned itself after the
Roman law and earlier Greek ideals of equity, equality, citizens' rights,
and elected officials. While following Brehon Law, this warrior-king

strategically captured rulers of nine territories in Ireland, Britain, and France and exchanged these "hostages" who then pledged allegiance to his growing Irish kingdom.

When writing about ancient and medieval history, it can be challenging to authenticate the actual existence of people from a specific time, especially those for whom exists scant historical records. During my research, I was delighted to uncover an article written by a European academic who had discovered compelling biological evidence that supports the historical and genealogical existence of the warrior-king. The warrior-king's dominant gene pool is thought to extend to some twenty-percent of men in the northeast region of what is today, Northern Ireland.

This Age of Roman Re-conquest also highlights the conversion of Ireland to Christianity by the well-known Christian missionary and bishop, St. Patrick. It is also during this time that the first wooden-churches would populate the landscape of medieval Ireland. Unsurprisingly, there is a disputed ancestral line prior to this Age. Nevertheless, the differences are well-known and confidence is taken from expert analysts who provide valuable insight that supports the ancestral story of *The Adam Connection*. With every new generation, I can sense a growing momentum in support of my humankind connection theory.

King Niall of the Nine Hostages (Ninetieth Generation)

Niall was the one-hundred-twenty-sixth High King of Ireland. The name Niall signifies "a noble knight" or "champion." This name is the root of the surname O'Neill. He was born in AD 311 in Tara, Ireland, and died in AD 378. His reign is known mainly for two things. He was the first Monarch to consolidate the northern region of Ireland.

Second, his military ability led him to the Irish control of all of Alba (Gaelic name for Scotland), and a large part of Britain. He was the first to give the name Scotland to Scotia Minor. He was a stout, wise, and warlike prince, and fortunate in all his conquests and achievements and was therefore called, "Great." There is evidence that Niall was not only good looking, but extremely intelligent. The Annals of the Four Masters regarded Niall as the "greatest warrior produced by Ireland at that time."

While Niall's combat training would have been very intense, he is credited with proficiency in written and spoken Latin. He was also called Naoi-Ghiallach or "Niall of the Nine Hostages." He got this title by taking royal hostages and securing loyalty from the nine provinces, regions, tribes, and countries he conquered and made part of his Kingdom. These included the four Irish provinces of Munster, Leinster, Connacht, and Ulster as well as his conquests in Brittany and tribal confederations including the Dalriads, Saxons, and Morini (a tribe in northern France). It is considered that the size of the Irish nation doubled under the rule of Niall. The Celtic methodology for subjugating nations followed Brehon Law, and would have governed the exchange of royal hostages for allegiance to the growing Irish nation. Brehon Law, also known as Early Irish Law, comprised the statutes which governed everyday life in Medieval Ireland.

Although the Roman Empire was already beginning to decline because of Emperor Constantine's efforts to quell rebellions in Spain, the raids and military excursions by Niall and his armies did much to weaken the power of Rome in Britain and France. Archeologists do not dispute Irish settlements in Wales, Cornwall, Scotland, and in Brittany (France).

Ireland has one of the oldest surname traditions in the world. Whereas in other countries names reflect professions or townlands, Irish surnames refer to ancestors. Traditionally, surnames are passed from father to child. The handing-down of this outward symbol of family is mirrored exactly by the genetic transmission of Y-chromosomes from fathers to sons. This genetic inheritance forms an unbroken chain from the past to the present.

In a survey of Y-chromosomes of Irish Dál Riata men, Professor Dan Bradley of Trinity College Dublin showed a small number of Y-chromosome types predominate in Ireland. In particular, one of these Y-chromosomes is very common in the northwest, being found in about one in five men there. The close genetic relationship of these Y-chromosomes to each other suggests a single origin—one or more dominant males. This geographic area coincides with the ancestral seat that can genetically trace back to Niall of the Nine Hostages. This genetic evidence gives independent support for the authenticity of historical and genealogical records. It is also strong evidence for long-lasting dominance of a single male lineage in medieval Ireland. Although some modern scholars may cast doubt about the historical existence of Niall of the Nine Hostages, Irish clans today relate back to the clearly dominant clan of Niall.[45],[46]

Much like the domination of Genghis Khan which left a legacy of 10 per cent of men in the region of Mongolia and 1 percent worldwide sharing a single Y-chromosome, Niall of the Nine Hostages has left a strong genetic imprint on modern Ireland and their descendants around the world.

Not only are scientists using carbon dating on historical artifacts, they are now using genetics to verify the person as well. In this case, it was the body of Niall himself. When the Irish raided the west coast of

---

[45] Aoife McLysaght, *The Genetic Imprint of Niall of the Nine Hostages*, Irish Times.

[46] Clayton N. Donoghue, The Irish Empire, The Story of Niall of the Nine Hostages, (Friesen Press, Victoria, Canada), 182.

Britain, they found what was undeniably that of Niall himself. British scholars believe a mass portion of the western coast line was suddenly inhabited by thousands of Irish immigrants in a short period of just twenty-five years. This migration pattern clearly implicates that the lands were taken by force. By conventional understanding, the land was conquered.

Prior to Niall, the kingdom of Ireland comprised the region of Ireland plus a small holding in southwest Wales and southwest Scotland. Immediately after Niall, the kingdom was more than double its size, including all of Scotland, half of Wales, all of Cornwall, and all of Brittany (Britain and France). Considering all the evidence that has been presented, the Irish under Niall did indeed once control an Empire.

His first wife was Inne, with whom he had five sons named Fergus, Enna, Aongus, Ualdhearg, and Fergus Altieathan. His second wife was Roigneach, with whom he had seven sons named Laeghire II, Conall, Crimthann, Conall Gulban, Fiacha, Main, Cairbre (ruler of the Chariot), and Eoghan.

King Eoghan Find
(Ninety-first Generation)

Eoghan was born in AD 337 in Ireland. The name Eoghan signifies "a young man" or "a youthful warrior." The anglicized name is either Eugene or Owen. Eoghan died in AD 405 in Ireland. He was converted to Christianity and baptized by St. Patrick at the Grianan Aileach, and his foot was pierced by the ornamental staff during the ceremony. The Grianan of Aileach is a group of historic structures atop a large hill in County Donegal. St. Patrick is generally considered to have led the conversion of Ireland to Christianity and during the fifth century AD, a strong monastic tradition developed. Eoghan married Muirchertach

Indorba. She was born AD 311 in Londonderry, Ireland. She died in Charlevoix, France. King Eoghan Find and Muirchertach Indorba had a son named Eochaidh Muinreamhar.

King Eochaidh Muinreamhar
(Ninety-second Generation)

Eochaidh was King of Dál Riata, born in Ulster, Ireland and died in AD 439 in Ireland. He married Loarn Erca. She was born in Ulster, Ireland, and died in Galicia, Spain. She was the daughter of King Loarn of Dál Riata in Scotland. Earca was a descendant of the Jewish matrilineal lineage found among Picts royalty.

There is some confusion as to whether Eochaidh was the son of Eoghan Find or Aengus Fear, who descended from a disputed blood line from a previous twenty-three generations, as noted by seventeenth century historian Matthew Kennedy in his book, *A Chronological and Historical Dissertation of the Royal Family of the Stuarts (1705)*. The seventeenth century chronicles of medieval Irish history, *Annals of the Four Masters*, suggest that Eochaid may have been the same person as Muiredach mac Eógain (Muiredach, the son or descendent of Eógain) and thus, belonged to the Uí Néill clan descended from Niall and Eoghan. The historical reliability and usefulness of various *Irish Chronicles* and *Annals* has sometimes been questioned by scholars.

Since these sources were limited to accounts of the births, deaths, and activities of the Irish nobility, they often ignored wider social trends or events that may have been prevalent at the time. This ignorance would be reasonable given the limited independent social communications institutions that would not have been in place during medieval times. On the other hand, *The Annals of the Four Masters* is considered a well-researched classic, representing one of the few written sources that provided valuable insight into famous people and events during this period of history. It is certainly possible that unrelated people or those only related through marriage, could have been worked into a single genealogical scheme that made descendants of the same legendary founder. Nevertheless, pragmatism reasonably justifies that this generation was Eochaidh, and with his wife Earca, they had a son named Ercc (Earc) Maceochaid.

King Ercc MacEochaid
(Ninety-third Generation)

Ercc was the King of Dál Riata who reigned for thirty-five years. He was born in AD 400 and died in AD 474 in Dál Riata, Ulster Ireland. He married Mist Ingen Loran. She was born in AD 412 and died in Dál Riata, Argyll, Scotland. It was in the year AD 439, Argyll became the dwelling place of the first Scots, meaning they were the first people to establish this dwelling place following dispossession by previous generations of Britons and Romans. Ercc flourished during the time of three Irish Kings.

Ercc's cousin, King Laeghaire, the one-hundred-twenty-eighth High King of Ireland, was a son of Niall of the Nine Hostages and the first Christian King. Laeghaire was converted from Paganism by St. Patrick. In his reign, Pope Celestinus I sent Palladius to Ireland to spread the faith among the Irish people. Palladius erected three wooden churches and left behind his books and a shrine with relics of Paul, Peter, and many martyrs.

King Oiloll Molt, the one-hundred-twenty-ninth High King of Ireland, reigned for twenty years and was slain in battle by the son of Laeghaire. King Lughaidh, the one-hundred-thirtieth High King of Ireland, was the son of Laeghaire, and during his reign, Ercc's son, Fergus

Mor MacEarca moved the throne of Dál Riata to Scotland. Legend has it that Lughaidh was killed by a flash of lightning, a miracle of God, because of his insult to St. Patrick.

Ercc and his wife Mist Ingen Loran, had twelve sons, three of which were named Loarn, Oengus, and Fergus Mor Mac Earca. From their son, Fergus Mor, descended the kings of Scotland. Through his descendent, Matilda, came the kings of England, including the royals' houses of Plantagenet and Stuart.

The next age spans three and one-half centuries, and begins with the birth of a young lad who became the patriarch of an ancient kingdom. Christianity continued to spread throughout the region and religion began to transform the people and their culture into a more civilized society. Mind you, battles for sovereign rule continued, but perhaps now with a more divine purpose. The last descendant of this age became the father of the first king of a "united" Scotland. Transcending these exciting developments was the birth of a prophet, some three-thousand miles from Scotland, who became the founder of a new monotheist religion. This next age brings the early stages of medieval history to life with the formation of a series of religious, cultural, and institutional "firsts" that would powerfully shape the world to come.

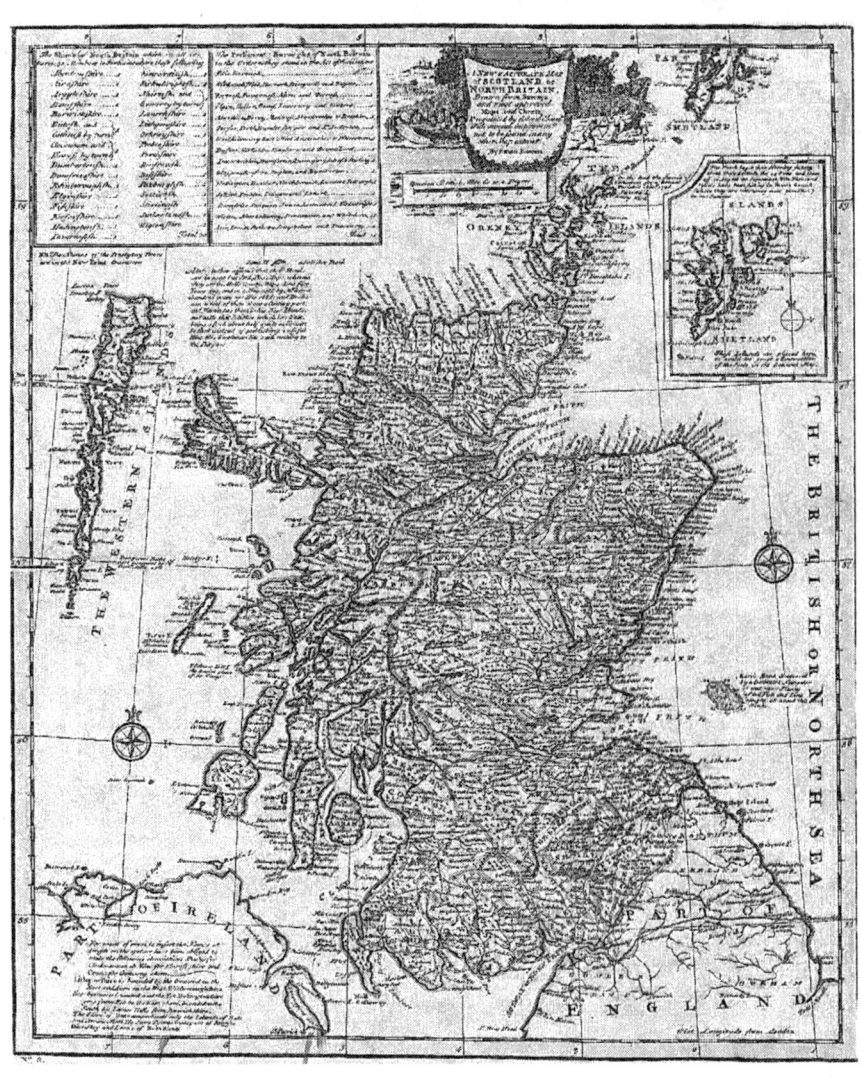

A New and Accurate Map of Scotland or North Britain by Emmanuel Bowen (1752). Courtesy Library of Congress Geography and Maps Division. This is the ancient kingdom of provincial kings who ruled until the birth of the Scottish monarchy.

Chapter 10

The Age of Scottish Monarchy (AD 462)

The next twelve generations extend over a period of nearly three-hundred-fifty years, in what I am calling The Age of Scottish Monarchy. This period originates with a patriarch who became the first monarch of an ancient Gaelic kingdom and an extraordinary founder of what would become the Scottish monarchy. In some respects, the patriarch was non-descript, were it not for his astonishing unification of disparate territories in southeast Scotland. On the surface, it is difficult to understand the cohesive force that bound together these lands, considering the difficult terrain separating these distant areas of Scotland.

Undoubtedly, the unification of this region over the next three centuries is only partially explained by self-determining violence and power that would force people to unite. However, most Scots believed it was the advent of Christianity that provided cohesion for transforming savages to civilized men and women. It was the Irish Abbott and missionary, Saint Columba, who in the sixth century would begin to spread the gospel of Jesus Christ and help create religious and political institutions that would provide structure, moral, and ethical rules that would govern a newly enlightened society.

However, this period was only the beginning of an emerging civil society. While the patriarch was a prestigious statesman with influential relationships back in Ireland, the settlers in this region were generally ferocious by nature. It was the savage killing of the patriarch's eighth great-grandson that would finally unite Scotland under what historians consider the first king of Scotland.

I found myself both encouraged by an emerging civilized nation and discouraged by the violence, battles, and savagery of humankind in this part of the world. While terribly interesting, I must wonder if this paradox of battles and blessings would continue to be the norm throughout all ages. In the same time that Columba spread Christianity in Scotland, the prophet Muhammed set out to unite the Arabian tribes in the Middle East and convert them from paganism to a new monotheist religion called Islam. After his death, the nations of Islam would strike out against Christianity and foreshadow religious wars throughout the Middle East and Europe, including the new kingdom of Scotland.

King Fergus Mor MacEarca
(Ninety-fourth Generation)

Fergus Mor Mac Earca was the first King of Dál Riata and founder of the Scottish monarchy. The name Fergus is known as "a strong warrior." He was born in the Gaelic Kingdom of Dál Riata, Argyllshire, Scotland, and died in AD 529 in Icolmkill (Iona) Island, Scotland. He married Feldelm Foltchain, daughter of Brion, King of Connaught and brother of Niall of the Nine Hostages. She was born in AD 475 in Leinster and died in AD 518.

Fergus established himself in Kintyre, Scotland and his brother Loarn in the region of Oban, Scotland. His brother Angus settled in Jura, Scotland. Their kingdoms were very small, but even so the patrimony of Fergus was soon divided between his two grandchildren, Comgall whose name survives in Cowal (near Dunoon) and his other grandson, Gabhran (from whom the Royal House of Scotland descends) in Knapdale, Scotland. The rock fortress of Dunadd was the capital, but the kings quarreled among themselves and possibly would have succumbed to the Picts had they not possessed a rudimentary Christianity and received reinforcements from Ireland. The advent of Columba in AD 563 had a political as well as religious consequence. Saint Columba was an Irish abbot and missionary who is widely credited with spreading Christianity in Scotland.

To the people of Scotland, it was perhaps the advent of Christianity that gave a new cohesion. It was the advocates of different types of Christianity who all taught the same great truths that brought to these savage folks a higher character and a better way of life.

It was also a function of Fergus' prestige, personality, and statesmanship which strengthened the Scots to resist the Picts and united them under the rule of Aidan of the house of Gabhran.[47] The son of Fergus and Feldelm was Domangart Reiti.

Domangart Reiti
(Ninety-fifth Generation)

Domangart was the second King of Dál Riata. He was born in AD 472 in Isleworth, England, and died in AD 534 in Dál Riata, Argyllshire, Scotland. He married Fedelmia Foltchain in Scotland. She was born in AD 434 in Ireland and died in AD 512 in Scotland. The children of Domangart and Fedelmia were named Gabhra, Eochaidh, Comgall, Goranus, and Gabran.

---

[47] Mary Elizabeth Eyer, *A Short History of Scotland*

King Gabhra Kynnatell
(Ninety-sixth Generation)

Gabhra Kynnatell was the fifth King of Dál Riata. He was born in AD 500 in Isleworth, England, and died in AD 560 in Dál Riata, Scotland. Scottish historians differ from the Irish analysts in that Gabhra is the son of Domangart instead of the grandson. He married Ada Lleian Ambrosius. She was born in AD 446 in Scotland and died in AD 532 in Dál Riata, Scotland. Gabhra and Ada had five sons, the eldest of which was Edhan Aidanus.

King Edhan Aidanus
(Ninety-seventh Generation)

Edhan Aidanus was the seventh King of Dál Riata and reigned for thirty-four years. He was born in AD 532 in Dál Riata, Scotland, and died April 17, 608 in Dál Riata, Scotland. Saint Columba, the Irish Abbot and missionary credited with spreading Christianity in Scotland, exhorted at the king's coronation that adversaries should never prevail against the new king (Edhan). Columba founded the abbey on Iona which became the dominant religious and political institution in the region for centuries. His nine sons were Arthur, Eochafin, Domangard, Tuathal, Conang, Brian (Bernard), Gartnad, Boetan, and Eochaidh Buidhe.

King Eochaidh Buidhe
(Ninety-eighth Generation)

Eochaidh Buidhe was the eighth King of Dál Riata. He was born in Scotland and died in AD 629 in Dál Riata, Scotland. He married Thurida. She was born in AD 570 in Dál Riata, Scotland, and died in AD 629 in Scotland. Eochaidh and Thurida had eight sons, one of whom was Domnall Brecc.

King Domnall Brecc
(Ninety-ninth Generation)

Domnall (Donald) was born about AD 600 in Dál Riata, Scotland, and died in AD 673 in Dál Riata, Scotland. Nicknamed "The Freckled," Domnall reigned for thirteen years. He headed an army of foreigners into Ireland in AD 637 in a dispute with the son of Domnall, the on-hundred-forty-sxith High King of Ireland. During his excursions to Ireland, Domnall fought and lost a seven-day battle at Mag Rathy (Moira, County Down). In his last battle, Domnall was slain by Hoan, King of the Britons. Domnall had sons Malduin and Domangart.

It was during the reign of Domnall that another religion was birthed in the Middle East. Born in AD 570 in Mecca, Muhammad ibn Abdallah worked as a merchant and shepherd before becoming discontent with secular life and retired to a life of religious meditation. It was about AD 610 in Arabia that Allah sent the prophet Muhammad to unite the Arabian tribes and turned them from idolatry to Islam. He received a series of divine revelations which became known as the Quran, the central religious text of Islam. Muhammad preached a monotheistic faith based on a complete submission to Allah. Muslims believe Islam is the original religion since the creation of Adam, the first prophet.

Since the beginning, all people who submit to Allah have been called Muslims and they believe Allah appointed thousands of prophets over the centuries including Abraham, Moses, David, and Jesus. After the death of Muhammed in AD 632, Islam rapidly spread throughout the Middle East and Europe. To Muslims, military and economic expansion of Islam liberated people suffering under corrupt empires from the past and this ideology led to numerous religious wars with Christians during the next several centuries. Muhammad's ascension and Islamic expansion foreshadowed the 200-year religious wars known as the Crusades, sanctioned by the Catholic Church, beginning in the eleventh century AD.

Domangart
(100th Generation)

Domangart was born AD 630 and died in AD 692 in Scotland. His son was Eochaid.

King Eochaid MacDomangart
(101st Generation)

Eochaid Mac Domangart was a King of Dál Riata who was born about AD 630 and died in AD 697. He married Spondana, daughter of King Macentfidich of the Picts. The Picts are those who occupied the extreme north and northeast of Scotland. Picts may have only been a nickname given in the third century by Roman soldiers to their painted adversaries who for so long resisted the expansion of Rome into Scotland. There is no doubt by historians that the Picts were the first people to inhabit the land in Scotland and noted for their matrilineal descent in the Royal House. Spondana was born in AD 660 in Perth, Scotland, and died in AD 697 in Dál Riata, Scotland. Their son was Eochaid.

King Eochaid MacEochaid
(102nd Generation)

Eochaid Mac Eochaid was King of Dál Riata who was born in AD 695 in Scotland, and died in AD 733. His son was Aodh Hugh Fionn.

Aodh Fionn "The Fair"
(103rd Generation)

Aodh Fionn was born about AD 720 in Dunolly Castle, Dál Riata, Scotland, and died in AD 778 in Dál Riata, Scotland. Aodh, anglicized as Hugh, is one of the most frequent names of the kings and chiefs of Ireland. He married Fergina, who was born in AD 727 in Perth, Scotland. She died in Scotland. Their eldest son was Fergus, King of Dál Riata and another son was named Eochaid.

King Eochaid MacAodh
(104th Generation)

Eochaid was the twentieth King of Dál Riata. He was born AD 776 in Dun Ollaigh Castle, Dál Riata, Scotland, and died AD 819 in Dál Riata, Scotland. He married Urgusa, the daughter of Hungus, King of the Picts. She was born about AD 755 in Scotland, and died in AD 803. Their children were Duncan D. Eryvine and Alpin.

King Alpin MacEochaid
(105th Generation)

Alpin was the twenty-second King of Dál Riata and reigned just fourteen years. He was born about AD 778 in the parish and village of Fordoun, in Kincardineshire, Scotland, and died on July 20, 834 in Galloway, Dumfrieshire, Scotland. He and many of his nobility and gentry were slain in battle by the Picts at a place called Bas-Alpin, meaning the death of Alpin. The Picts were so savagely cruel that they carried the head of Alpin in triumph and in public view. Privately, certain resolute young men, including his son and successor, rewarded the nation bountifully, when by the hand of God, they overpowered the whole nation and revenged the death of Alpin. Before his death, Alpin had married Unistic, Princess of the Picts. The children of Alpin and Unistic were Gregor, Domnall, Mailmara, and Kenneth.

The next seven centuries represent a period of dramatic developments in Scottish and European history. The first Scottish ruler in this next age will be followed by bloodline descendants, not all of whom would lead an often fractured, yet powerful sovereign nation. As we transition during this time from Medieval to early Modern history, people and institutions are torn-apart by a movement that reshapes political and religious power structures throughout Europe.

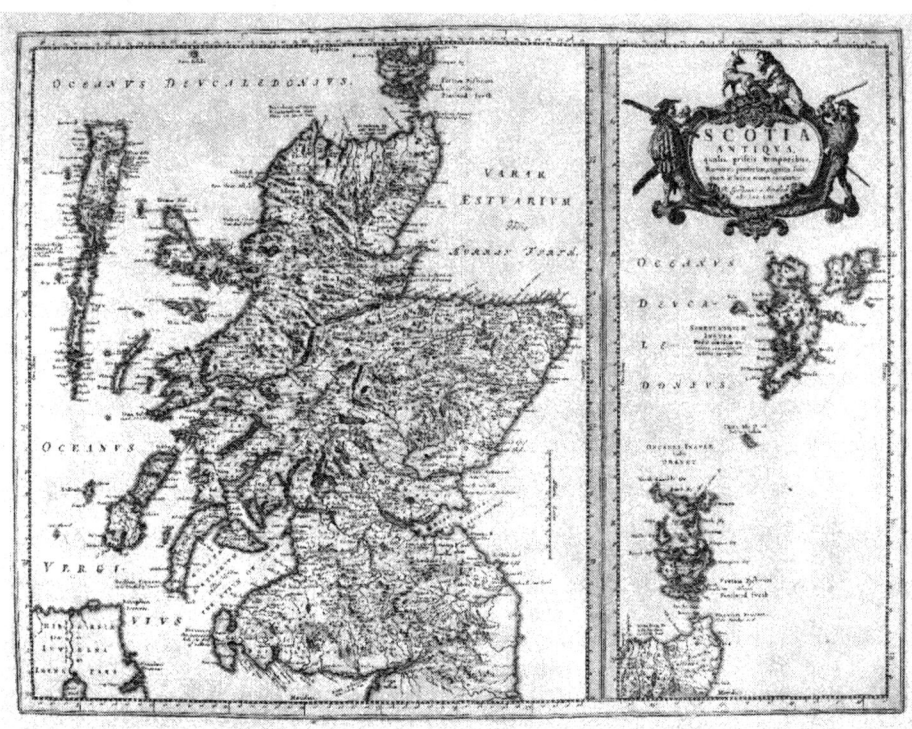

Antique Map of Scotland by R. Gordonius (1654). The Island of Iona on the Western coast of Scotland is where the first king of Scotland was born. Iona was the center of Gaelic monasticism during the previous four-hundred years before the birth of the Scottish monarchy.

Chapter 11

The Age of Scottish Kings (AD 810)

The next twenty-five generations extend over a period of more than seven-hundred-fifty years in this Age of Scottish Kings. Like other ages of *The Adam Connection*, this period begins with a powerful man who unites an ancient Gaelic kingdom and tribal confederation to become the first King of "Albany," the Gaelic name for Scotland. This father of Scottish kings was swept into power by revenging the brutal death of his father in the previous generation.

During this Age, there were many noteworthy events within and outside of Scotland that shaped the monarchy and successive generations. We learn about the seventh great-grandson of the first Scottish king who successfully implored the nobility council to change the basis for Crown succession to that of heredity. During this Age of Scottish Kings, we learn about the first instance of a matrilineal bloodline succession in more than five-thousand-years, and would repeat itself an additional seven times until present day.

During this time, the first Scottish king instituted new titles such as "Earls" and "Barons" for royal family members. A royal title translated as "Steward" becomes the basis for a royal dynasty that descended from this Age of Scottish Kings. During this tumultuous age, an estimated forty million people in Europe, more than one-third of the population, died of the bubonic plague.

The same advent of Christianity in the Scottish kingdom would clash with the arrival of Islam in the Middle East, resulting in the first and second crusades where the Scots and English fought Muslims in the name of Jesus Christ. In truth, these Crusades were about religious and political power within the Holy Roman Empire. As if this Age of Scottish Kings was not interesting enough, the clash of politics and religion continued in the form of the Protestant Reformation.

It was in the early sixteenth century that a quiet, scholarly monk in Germany ignited a political and religious firestorm that consumed Scotland, Europe, and the entire world. Towards the end of this era of Scottish Kings, fierce opposition arose from a Protestant leader in Scotland who vigorously attacked the "divine legitimacy" of female monarchs in Scotland and England. The rule and power of the Catholic Church would forever change at the end of this era, and yet Christianity would expand and influence the world culture as never before in history. The theme of battles and blessings continues.

King Kenneth MacAlpin
(106th Generation)

Kenneth was the first King of Scotland. He was King of Dál Riata from 839–841; King of the Picts as Kenneth III from 841–843, and Kenneth I of Scotland from 842–858. Kenneth was born in 810 in Iona, Scotland, and died February 13, 858, in the Palace of Cinnbelachoir, in Perth, Scotland. During his sovereignty, he made a union between Dál Riata and the Pict nation and was the first Scottish King of Albany, the archaic name for modern day Scotland.

The total area of modern day Scotland is approximately 30,000 square miles with more than a tenth lying in scattered islands, many of which abound in rocks and mosses. The land mass is beautified with mountains, lochs (lakes), and moors. Moors are neither forested cultivated. In the highlands, moors are characterized by high rainfall, acidic soil, and low lying sparse vegetation.

King Kenneth MacAlpin also battled the Scandinavian marauders and Anglo-Saxons invading northward from England. After Iona had been repeatedly ransacked by the Norsemen, the religious capital of Scotland moved first to Dunkeld and later to St. Andrews. Kenneth must have known that a factor in the unification of Scotland was the fortunate geography of Pictland being far removed from the south, and her east coast proved to be far less attractive to the Scandinavians then the indented and island scattered west coast.

During the reign of Kenneth, poor peasants who left the barren soil of western Norway, met little opposition in their migration to sparsely populated outlying areas of Shetland, Orkney, Caithness, Sutherland, the Western Isles, the Isle of Man, and parts of Ross. In addition to battles with the Norse, links between Kenneth's kingdom and Ireland were weakened as was his relationship with southern England and the continent.

In the face of this, Kenneth and his successors were forced to consolidate their position in their kingdom, and the union between the Picts and the Gaels, already progressing for several centuries, began to strengthen. By the time of Donald II, the kings would be called kings neither of the Gaels or the Scots but of Alba. Notwithstanding the Norse incursions, historians generally agreed that Alpin enlarged his dominions and it is believed that during his time, school learning flourished in the region.[48]

Kenneth married Aelgigu (Leinster) of Scotland and then Hunrfrd (of Ossory). His son was Constantine.

King Constantine I
(107th Generation)

Constantine was the third King of Scotland and reigned for fourteen years (862–876), succeeding his brother, Donald. He was crowned at Scone, upon the Stone of Destiny, after he conquered the Picts, who had invited the Danes into Albany, hoping that their alliance would rescue the sovereignty out of the hands of the Albanian Scots. The Danes had infiltrated the country during his reign. At the battle fought near Dollar, Scotland, the Picts suffered a heavy defeat and King Constantine was slain in battle, perhaps by beheading on a Fife beach. It was also during this time that Constantine built a new church for the Christian monastic community at St. Andrews.

Constantine was born about 836 in Scotland and died in 877 in the parish of Inverdovat in Fifeshire, Scotland. His son was Donald II.

King Donald II "The Madman"
(108th Generation)

Donald was the sixth King of Scotland and reigned from 889-900. He was born about 862 in Scotland and died in 900 in the village of Forres in Morayshire, Scotland. He was slain by his cousin, Constantine II, during a Danish invasion. His son was Malcom.

---

[48] J.D. Mackie, *A History of Scotland*, (Penguin Books, London, England), 18, 24.

King Malcom I
(109th Generation)

Malcom was the eighth King of Scotland and reigned for eleven years from 943-954. He briefly was King of England in 945. He died in 954 in the village of Fordoun in Kincardineshire, Scotland. His son was Kenneth.

King Kenneth II
(110th Generation)

Kenneth was the thirteenth King of Scotland and reigned for twenty-four years from 971-995. He was born about 954 in the island of Iona in Argyll, Scotland, and put to death by his own subjects in AD 995. Iona is an island off the western coast of Scotland and since the sixth century AD had become a center of Irish-influenced monasticism which expanded into northern England, Scotland, and France. During his reign, Kenneth called a Council of the Nobility at Scone, where after debating the inconveniences of attending the ancient customs of electing their kings, he obtained their consent to make the Crown hereditary. His wife was Auligigu daughter of Duncan Mac Donnachadh, Duke and Earl of Caithness. She was born in 920 and died in 958 in the ancient County of Caithness in Highland, Scotland. Their son was Malcolm II.

King Malcolm II
(111th Generation)

Malcom II was sixteenth King of Scotland and ruled for twenty-nine years from 1005-1034. He was born in 958 in Perth, Scotland, and died on November 25, 1034, at Glamis Castle in Angus, Scotland. Since Malcolm had no son of his own who could descend to the throne, he commenced a series of dynastic marriages of his three daughters to men who might otherwise be his rival to the throne. He first married his daughter Bethoc (Beatrix) to Crinan, Thane of The Isles, head of the house of Atholl and secular Abbot of Dunkeld. His youngest daughter, Olith was married to Sigurd, Earl of Orkney. His middle daughter, Donada, was married to Finlay, Earl of Moray, Thane of Ross and Cromarty and a descendant of Loarn of Dál Riata.

Donada was mother of Macbeth, the grandson of Kenneth II and King of Scotland from 1040-1057. The play, *The Tragedy of Macbeth* by William Shakespeare, is thought to have been first performed in 1606, and dramatized the damaging physical and psychological effects of political ambition on those who seek power for its own sake. It is from his first daughter Beatrix that this ever so brief matrilineal bloodline continued.

Beatrix
(112th Generation)

Beatrix was a Princess of Scotland. She was born in 984 in Perthshire, Scotland, and died in 1045 in the small town of Dunkeld in Perthshire, Scotland. It was in 1010 at the town of Atholl, Perthshire, Scotland, where Beatrix married Crinan De Mormaer, son of Lord Duncan Mormaer, lay Abbott of Dunkeld and Lord of Isles. Crinan was born in 980 in Atholl, Scotland, and slain in 1045 in Dunkeld, Scotland. Their son was Duncan.

King Duncan I
(113th Generation)

Duncan I was the seventeenth King of Scotland and ruled from 1034–1040. He was born in 1013 in Perth, Scotland, and died on

The Age of Scottish Kings (AD 810)

August 14, 1040, in the cathedral city of Elgin, Moray, Scotland. During his reign, the north and west of Scotland was conquered by the Norse, under the leadership of Thorfinn, Jarl (Chief) of the Orkney Islands in the northern isles of Scotland.

In 1030, Duncan married Sibyle Fitzsiward, daughter of Siward Biornsson, whose parents were the Earl Northumbria and Aelfled Elfleda, Countess of Bernicia. Sibyle was born in 1014 in Northumberland, England, and died in 1040 in Iona, Scotland. Duncan was put to death by his first cousin, MacBeth, who succeeded him as King. Duncan and Sibyle's children were Duncan, Donald, David, Margaret, and Malcolm III.

King Malcolm III
(114th Generation)

Malcolm III was the twenty-first King of Scotland who reigned for thirty-six years from 1057-1093. He was born on March 26, 1031, in Atholl, Scotland, and died on November 13, 1093, in Alnwick Castle, Northumberland, England. He killed MacBeth in 1057, in the village of Lumphanan in Aberdeenshire, Scotland. Malcolm was the first Scottish King who created titles of Earls and Barons for the Royalty and amongst the natives, the honorable titles of More-Mhoer and Thane. It is from the word More-Mhoer, signifying Steward, that the surname of the family of Stuart is derived and fully established in the annals of history to present days.

In 1068, Malcolm III married Margaret, daughter of Edward Aethling and Agatha von Brunswick of the Royal House of Wessex. She was a granddaughter of Edmund "Ironsides," the King of England who resisted a Danish invasion in 1015. Edmund was placed in the catalog of Saints by Pope Clement X. Margaret was the seventh in descent from Alfred the Great, King of Wessex who reigned from 871-899. Wessex was the Anglo-Saxon kingdom in south and west England that had become the dominant English power before unification of the country. Alfred successfully defended his kingdom against the Viking invasion and became the dominant ruler of England. Margaret was born on September 8, 1045, in Wessex, England, and died on November 16, 1093, in Castle Edinburgh, Scotland. Their children were Edgar, King of Scotland; Alexander, Matilda, Duncan II, Mary Countess of Boulogne, Edmund, Ethelred, and David.

King David I "The Saint"
(115th Generation)

David, the twenty-eighth King of Scotland, reigned for thirty-one years from 1124-1153. He was born in 1080 in Edinburgh, Scotland, and died on May 24, 1153, in Carlisle, England. During his reign, the First Crusade in Europe, a religious Holy war, ended in 1099, after the recapture of Jerusalem and the brutal massacre of Jewish and Muslim occupants. The Second Crusade that ended in 1146, was in response to the Muslim conquest of Edessa, the crusade capital today known as Turkey.

David was one of medieval Scotland's greatest ecclesiastical leaders. It was in 1113 that David, as Prince of the Cumbrians, created Selkirk Abbey and founded more than a dozen new monasteries during his reign. Around 1115 when he was the only ruler of Strathclyde, David founded and richly endowed the Diocese of Glasgow. Before his death, David had created or restored Bishops in Galloway, Moray, Dunkeld, Ross, Caithness, Aberdeen, Dunblane, and Brechin. The association of Royalty with the well-organized Scottish church, spread religion and conveyed social as well as spiritual benefits.

During the reigns of his elder brothers, Edgar and Alexander, David lived with his sister Matilda in England. In the latter part of 1113, King

Henry of England gave David the hand of Matilda of Huntingdon. Matilda was the widow of Simon de Senlis and daughter and heiress of Waltheof, Earl of Northumberland. Matilda was the heiress to the expansive territory in Huntingdon and Northampton. Upon Alexander's death, David and Matilda returned to Scotland where he was proclaimed King with great joy.

David's impact on Scottish cultural development was significant, and he is often known as David "The Saint." He continued his brother's introduction of religious and political reforms by founding monasteries and the royal boroughs of Stirling, Perth, Dunfermline, and Edinburgh. He also introduced a feudal system and granted land to Anglo-Norman immigrants who anglicized the Scottish Lowlands. The Royal court spoke in English while Gaelic was spoken in the Highlands and Norse in the North and Scottish Isles.

David became involved in the struggle for succession in England, and supported the succession of Henry I's daughter the Empress Matilda. When Stephen usurped her, and became king, David invaded England in 1138 and conquered Carlisle and Newcastle before being defeated in the battle of the Standard near Northallerton in Yorkshire, England, in 1138. When Stephen faced his own struggles in England, the Crown granted David control of Northumbria under the Treaty of Durham in 1139 and recognized him as king of an independent Scotland. David and Matilda had a son Malcom, who was strangled by his great uncle Donald Bane and another son named Henry.

Henry
(116ᵗʰ Generation)

Henry was the seventh Earl of Huntingdon. He was born in 1114 in the town of Kelso in Roxburghshire, Scotland. He died on June 12,

1152, in Kelso, Scotland. It was in 1139 in Warwick, England, that Henry married Ada, Countess of Warenne, who was the daughter of William II de Warenne, the second Earl of Surrey, and his wife Isabel Elizabeth de Vermandois, Countess of Leicester. William de Warenne was a grandson of William the Conqueror. Ada was born in 1120 in the County of Surrey in Kent, England. She died in 1178 in Huntingdon, England. Their children were daughters Margaret and Alda, and sons Malcolm, William, and David. Margaret was married to Conangus, Duke of Brittany in France, and Alda was married to Florence, Earl of Holland.

David
(117th Generation)

David was the eighth Earl of Huntington in England. He was born in 1144 and died in 1219. During his generation, The Third Crusade that ended in 1192, was led by Richard the Lion-Heart, King of England, along with Philip II of France, and Barbarossa the Holy Roman Emperor. The Crusade captured Cyprus, Acre, and Jaffa, with Richard negotiating access to Jerusalem for Christians. David was married in 1190 to Matilda (Maud), daughter of Hugh Kevlioch, third Earl of Chester. She was born in 1171 and died in 1233. Their children were Margaret, Robert, Ada, Matilda (Maud), John (Earl of Huntingdon), Henry, and Isobel.

Isobel
(118th Generation)

Isobel was born in 1199 in the town of Huntingdon, Cambridgeshire, England, and died in 1251 in England. She was married about 1208 to Robert Bruce, fourth Lord of Annandale. Through her came the claims of her son in 1290, and later in the beginning of the fourteenth century of her great-grandson, Robert the Bruce, seventh Lord of Annandale, to the Scottish throne. During Isobel's generation, it was in 1201 that Pope Innocent III claimed the right of the pope to oversee the moral conduct of heads of state and to choose rulers, including the emperor of Rome. This Isobel's children were Robert and Bernard. Robert, fifth Lord of Annandale was regent and recognized heir to the throne in the years just before her death.

Robert de Brus
(119th Generation)

Robert was fifth Lord of Annandale in England. He was born in 1210 in Annandale, Scotland, and died in 1295 in Priory, Scotland. Robert refused to agree to the Crown of Scotland in 1290 against Baliol, his first cousin, because he would not accept what he believed to be dishonorable terms set by King Edward, namely, subordinating Scotland to the Crown of England.

During the time of Robert de Brus, from around 1258-1273, the Italian philosopher and Dominican Monk, Thomas Aquinas, authored his two-best-known works, the *Summa contra Gentiles* and the *Summa Theologiae*. Recognized for his thoughts in uniting faith and reason, Thomas Aquinas is considered one of the most important philosophers in the history of Western Civilization and whose ideology still underpins Catholic doctrine and dogma. In 1265, Aquinas served as the papal theologian and taught the full range of philosophical subjects of both moral and natural natures. While teaching, Aquinas wrote his most famous work, *Summa Theologiae*, which he believed was useful for instructing beginning students in the doctrine of Catholic truth. Aquinas could not have known the insatiable desire of the everyday person to better understand biblical truth and how that desire and seeking of truth would lead some two-hundred-fifty years later to the schism between Catholicism and what would become known as Protestantism.

Despite pervasive conditions of violence and evil in the world at the time of Aquinas, he developed extensive philosophical ideas in *Summa contra Gentiles* including his definitive belief and understanding that God is immovable, that nothing can be violent in Him and there is therefore nothing in Him that is unnatural or violent. Aquinas was equally cogent in expressing his theological ideas in *Summa Theologiae*, including his clarity around the deficiency in man with respect to evil. His studied views forcefully declared that evil can only become a fault or consequence when man voluntarily acts upon things in the natural world and that evil never originates from God.

Robert de Bruce was married to Isabella of Gloucester and Hertford and after her death, married Christina, daughter of Sir William de Ireby and widow of Adam Jesmond, the Sheriff of Northumberland. He had ten children including Elizabeth, Ada, Christian, William, and Robert.

Robert Bruce
(120th Generation)

Robert Bruce was sixth Lord of Annandale and Earl of Carrick who lived from July 1243 to March 1304. He is mostly remembered as the father of a King of Scotland, Robert the Bruce, and of a King of Ireland, Edward Bruce. He married Marjorie, Countess of Carrick in 1271, and she died in 1292. She was the daughter of Neil, Earl of Carrick. Foreshadowing one of the undermining conditions that led to the sixteenth century Protestant Reformation, Pope Boniface VIII claimed supremacy over secular rulers throughout the Roman Catholic empire, including the nation of Scotland. The children from Robert and Marjorie were Edward (King of Ireland), Thomas, Alexander, Nigel, Isabel, Mary, Christian, Matilda, Margaret, and Robert.

King Robert the Bruce
(121st Generation)

Robert was King of Scotland for twenty-three years from 1306–1329. He was born on July 11, 1274, at Turnberry Castle in Ayrshire, Scotland, and died of a serious illness, possibly leprosy, on June 7, 1329, at his house in Cardross, Scotland.

While not part of this bloodline, the previous King of Scotland, Balliol, abdicated the throne in 1296. Hence, Scotland was without a monarch for ten years and ruled remotely by King Edward I of England. The Scots national resistance developed into a War of Independence from England, in which William Wallace and then Robert I played a leading role. Wallace won a victory over the English at Stirling Bridge in 1297, and proclaimed himself Guardian of Scotland. The following year Edward invaded Scotland again and defeated William Wallace at Falkirk.

A few weeks before his coronation, Robert killed his greatest rival for the crown, Sir John Comyn, in a Dumfries church, during the last of many arguments between them. For his murder of Sir Comyn, Robert was outlawed by Edward I and excommunicated by Pope Clement V.

On March 25, 1306, Robert officially took over the title of Guardian of Scotland and claimed the throne as the great-great grandson of David I. Determined to be made King in the ancient Scottish tradition, he hurried to Scone and was crowned by Isabella, Countess of Buchan, representing her brother the Earl of Fife. The Bishops of St. Andrews, Glasgow, Moray along with the Abbott of Scone were in attendance alongside of the newly crowned King. He was chosen to be King of

Scots and to lead the fight for Scottish independence against Edward I of England.

The War of Independence that began in 1298, was made easier by the death of Edward I as he set out to claim back Scotland. Bruce set about removing the English from Scotland and by early 1314, Stirling was the only castle in English hands.

In 1320, Bruce and the Scottish nobles issued the Declaration of Arbroath asserting Scottish Independence, "For as longs as one hundred of us shall remain alive we shall never in any wise consent to submit to the rule of the English, for it is not for glory that we fight, but for freedom alone." However, a truce with Edward II of England failed to stop hostilities which continued until Edward II was deposed in 1327.

The Treaty of Edinburgh between Robert I and Edward III in 1328, recognized Scotland's independence, ending the thirty-year War of Independence. Shortly thereafter, Edward agreed to the marriage of Robert Bruce's son David to his younger sister Joan, daughter of Edward II.

Robert first married Isabella of Mar when she was eighteen years old. She was the daughter of Domhnall, Earl of Mar, who was one of seven guardians of Scotland who believed Robert to be the legitimate King of Scotland. Despite considerable risks to his fortune, which proved to be true, the Earl of Mar arranged for Robert to marry his daughter, Isabella and was the first to sign over his family estates to Robert. Shortly after their marriage, Isabella became pregnant giving birth to a daughter, Marjorie Bruce, but died soon thereafter in 1296. Six years later, Robert married his second wife, Elizabeth de Burgh, and their children were David, John, Matilda, and Margaret plus several illegitimate children.

Princess Marjorie married Walter Stewart, sixth High Steward of Scotland, and their son became Robert II of Scotland. From him descend the monarchs of the House of Stewart and the later royal families of the United Kingdom.

Marjorie Bruce
(122nd Generation)

Marjorie, Princess of Scotland, was arranged to be married in 1315 to Walter Steward, sixth High Steward of Scotland. She was born in 1296 and died on March 2, 1316.

In June of 1306, just three months after her father's coronation, Marjorie was sent into hiding after Bruce and his army were defeated at the Battle of Methven. Shortly thereafter, ten-year-old Marjorie was captured and turned over to Edward I of England. She was exiled and confined to the convent at the market town of Watton, England, where she endured daily public humiliation for seven years until she was set free in 1314 by Edward II.

Two years later at Paisley Abbey, on March 2, 1316, Marjorie gave birth to her son Robert by Caesarean section after she went into premature labor after falling off a horse. Marjorie was just nineteen years old when she died within a few hours of childbirth. Her son, Robert II, succeeded his childless uncle David II of Scotland and became the first Stewart King.

King Robert II
(123rd Generation)

Robert Stewart II was King of Scotland for nineteen years from 1371-1390. He was born March 2, 1316, in Paisley, Scotland and died April 19, 1390, at Dundonald Castle in Ayrshire, Scotland. It was from 1348-1351 that the Bubonic plague, also known as Black Death, killed an estimated one-third of the people in Europe resulting in an estimated loss of forty million lives. People, in their insensible desperation, blamed the flea-transmitted disease on the Catholic Church, the Jews or personal immorality.

It was in England at the beginning of King Robert II's reign that English priest and diplomat, John Wycliffe, proposed limitations on papal taxation and civil powers. He challenged some church doctrines, most notably transubstantiation, which the Catholic Church teaches is the change of substance, by which the bread and wine offered in the sacrament of the Eucharist during Mass, become the actual body and blood of Jesus Christ. Wycliffe also believed that Scripture should be available to people in their own language, resulting in translation of the entire Bible into English from Latin in 1382, and it became known as the Wycliffe Bible.

Robert was the first Stewart King of what became known as *The House of Stuart*, a European royal dynasty that ascended to become Kings and Queens of Scotland, England, and Ireland until 1707, and then of Great Britain and Ireland until the death of Queen Anne in 1714.

In 1336, Robert married his first wife Elizabeth Mure, daughter of Sir Adam Mure of Rowaallan. Elizabeth was his mistress before she became Robert's wife and believed to have been an uncanonical union in the eyes of the Catholic Church. Robert and Elizabeth had ten children including John (Earl of Carrick), who became Robert III, King of Scotland.

After Elizabeth died and upon receiving Papal dispensation to marry a second time, Robert II married his second wife on May 2, 1355. Euphemia was the widow of John Randolph, Earl of Moray. Their children were David, Walter, Egidia, and Katherine. Robert II also had several illegitimate sons including John (Bute), Thomas (St. Andrews),

Alexander (Glasgow), John (Dundonald), Alexander (Inverlunan), James (Kinfauns), and John (Cardney).

Following the defeat by the English of his uncle David II at Halidon Hill, Scotland, Robert escaped and at the age of seventeen in 1333, took over as Guardian of Scotland while David was in exile in France. He ascended to the throne upon the death of David, and did not rule with authority over the nobles who were critical of his leadership. In order to restore law and order in the kingdom, his heir John (Robert III), took over the rule.

King Robert III
(124th Generation)

Robert Stewart III, was King of Scotland for sixteen years from 1390-1406. He was born on August 14, 1337, and died on April 4, 1406, at Dundonald Castle in Ayrshire, Scotland. He married Annabella Drummond in 1366.

Robert III was a timid man who became an invalid after being kicked by a horse in 1388. He took the name Robert because his name John was considered a bad omen after the hated Scottish King John Balliol endured a short, but difficult reign, caught between the English King and the Scottish nobles who humiliated him.

By 1398, Robert III's health was limiting his ability to rule so much that the Scottish Parliament appointed his oldest son, David Stewart, first Duke of Rothesay to be Lieutenant of the Kingdom. Robert III, now largely sidelined in his own kingdom, sought to protect his son, James Stewart by rallying support for him, making him Earl of Carrick, and making Stewart lands in the southwest into a separate principality for him. James was eventually captured by the English and put into exile. Upon Robert III's death and with James a captive of the English, the Scottish Parliament appointed Robert III's unscrupulous brother, Robert, Duke of Albany, as Governor and Regent of Scotland. The Duke of Albany was to retain the post until his death in 1420.

The children of Robert III and Anabella were David (Earl of Carrick), Robert, Margaret, Mary, Egidia, Elizabeth, and illegitimate sons James (Kilbride) and John (Shaw Stewart).

King James I Stewart
(125th Generation)

James was King of Scotland for thirty-one years from 1406-1437. He was born on July 25, 1394, at Dunfermline in Fife, Scotland, and died on February 21, 1437, when he was assassinated in Preachers, Scotland, by his uncle Walter, Earl of Atholl. It was during his reign that in 1408, it became illegal in England to translate or read the Bible in English without permission of a bishop. During 1414-1418, the ecumenical Council of Constance, recognized by the Catholic Church, rejected Wycliffe's teachings, and burned Jan Hus, the Czech priest, reformer, and philosopher, at the stake as a heretic.

James was a prisoner in England for nearly twenty years in the Tower of London. During that time, his uncle Robert of Albany ruled Scotland and did very little to secure James' release, instead hoping that his own son, Murdoch would assume the throne. James was Scotland's first renaissance prince, a patron of learning and culture, and stern judge and ruler. He was considered a strong leader and introduced much legislation for the social and economic benefits of Scotland. He also founded the Scottish Court of Session, the supreme civil court of Scotland that constitutes part of the College of Justice. The Court of Session sits in Parliament House in Edinburgh and is both a trial court and a court of appeal.

He married Joan Beaufort on February 13, 1424. Joan was the daughter of John Beaufort, Earl of Somerset, and niece of King Henry IV of England. Their children were Alexander (Duke of Rothesay), Margaret (Queen of France), Isabella, Jean, Eleanor, Mary, Annabella, and James II.

King James II Stewart
(126th Generation)

James II was King of Scotland for twenty-three years from 1437-1460. He was born on October 16, 1430, at Holyrood Abbey in Edinburgh, Scotland, and died on August 3, 1460, when he was killed in a cannon explosion at the battle of Roxburh in Scotland. During his reign in 1456, Johannes Gutenberg printed the Latin Vulgate, the first book printed using movable type. The invention made the Bible accessible to more people who previously could not afford hand printed copies.

James was just six-years old when he succeeded to the throne following the murder of his father. He was crowned at Holyrood Abbey ending the tradition since Kenneth MacAlpin of crowning at Scone. Unsurprisingly, William Crichton of Edinburgh, Alexander Livingstone of Stirling, and William Douglas fought for control of the throne as would not have been unusual in the early days of a child Monarch. However, the resourceful James and his consort took over power of the position when he had Livingstone arrested and is said to have personally killed William, Earl of Douglas in AD 1452. James' reign included the creation of new earldoms, organization of central government with taxing authority, and the founding of The University of Glasgow in 1451.

During the reign of James II, there was growing political and religious tension within the Holy Roman Empire. It was in 1440 that

Johannes Gutenberg invented the movable type printing press that spread to over two hundred cities in a dozen European countries during the next twenty years. The "Press" as it became known, was quickly used to disseminate ideas about all sorts of things, but mostly about religion. Gutenberg first produced a Bible using movable type in 1453. This key technology became an essential enabler of social, political, and religious discourse and upheaval that affected the next five generations of kings and queens in Scotland and England. It included the rise of the Protestant reformation that relied upon the new print culture originated by Gutenberg's invention.

Nearly 400 years later, Scottish philosopher Thomas Carlyle, one of the most influential commentators of his time, wrote in his book, *Sartor Resartus*, about Gutenberg and his invention: "He who first shortened the labor of copyists by device of movable types was disbanding hired armies, and cashiering most kings and senates, and creating a whole new democratic world: he had invented the art of printing."[49]

On July 3, 1449, James married Mary, daughter of Arnold, Duke of Gueldress. Their children were Alexander (Duke of Albany), David (Earl of Moray), John (Earl of Mar), Mary, Margaret, and James (Duke of Rothesay) who succeeded James II on the throne. He had one illegitimate son, Sir John of Sticks.

King James III Stewart
(127th Generation)

James III was King of Scotland for twenty-eight years from 1460-1488. He was born in May of 1452, and died at the Battle of Sauchieburn

---

[49] The Printing Press. *Lectures on Modern European Intellectual History*. The History Guide

on June 11, 1488, near Stirling, Scotland. James received the crown at the age of eight upon the death of his father, King James II. Scotland was governed first by James' mother, Mary of Gueldres who died in 1463, and James Kennedy, bishop of St. Andrews who died in 1465, and then by a group of nobles headed by the Boyds of Kilmarnock, who seized the king in 1466. In 1469, James overthrew the Boyds and began to govern for himself. Unlike his father, he was unable to restore strong central government.

Scottish nobles were disaffected by James' love of the arts and fondness for male friends. He was considered a weak and unpopular king, besieged by rebellions. In AD 1479, James arrested his brothers, Alexander, Duke of Albany, and John, Earl of Mar, on suspicion of treason. Two powerful border families, the Homes and the Hepburns, led an uprising in AD 1488 and won the support of James' fifteen-year-old son, the future King James IV.

In 1469, he married Margaret, who was daughter of King Christian I of Denmark and Norway. Their children were James (Marquess of Ormond, Duke of Ross, Archbishop of St. Andrews, Chancellor of Scotland), John (Earl of Mar), and James (Duke of Rothesay and future king).

King James IV Stewart
(128th Generation)

James IV was King of Scotland for twenty-five years from 1488-1513. He was born on March 17, 1473, and died on September 9, 1513, at the Battle of Flodden Field in Northumberland, England.

James IV was fifteen when his father was assassinated and was an unwilling participant in the rebellion that killed his father. He was considered a Renaissance King who spoke several languages including

Gaelic, English, and French, and enjoyed the arts and learning. He founded Aberdeen University, and after the printing press came to Scotland, he made education compulsory for barons and wealthy land-owners. In 1502, he created a truce "of perpetual peace" with England. A year later, in an act of reconciliation to bring the thrones of Scotland and England together, he married Princess Margaret Tudor, daughter of King Henry VII of England.

James and Margaret had two daughters who died in their infancy and sons James, Arthur, Alexander (Duke of Ross), and James (Duke of Rothesay) who ascended to the crown upon his father's death. James also had several illegitimate children including Alexander (Archbishop of St. Andrews), James (Earl of Moray), Catherine, Margaret, and Jean.[50]

King James V Stewart
(129th Generation)

James V was King of Scotland for twenty years from 1513-1542. He was born on April 10, 1512, at Linlithgow Palace in Scotland, and died on December 14, 1542, at Falkland Palace in Fife, Scotland.

James V was just over one-year old when his father was killed at Flodden field and he inherited the throne. Again, the Scottish nobles fought for power during the King's period of infancy where ultimately the kingdom was led by his mother Margaret and her second husband, Douglas, Earl of Angus

When James V escaped from his step-father's authority, he ruled with authority, but was compassionate to the poor of Scotland. It was during this time in history that Protestantism arose in Europe and England.

It was on October 31, 1517, that an obscure monk, Martin Luther, hammered his theological indictments of Catholicism to the door of

---

[50] www.britroyals.com

All Saints' Church in the small Saxon university town of Wittenberg, Germany. Luther did not intend to impugn the authority of the Pope, but his ninety-five Theses did just that by ultimately challenging and maligning Church leadership and rupturing the spiritual unity of medieval Europe. Martin Luther wanted reform, not Reformation. He is credited or blamed, depending on your perspective, with shattering Catholic dominion and plunging Europe into religious wars.

Pope Leo X, a kingpin of the powerful Italian Medici family and last Pope to have not been in Priestly orders at the time of his election, was unable to separate and reform the entangled relationships between Church and state throughout Europe. Luther attacked his policy of financing a new St. Peter's Church in Rome with indulgences, effectively cash payments, mainly from the poor, in exchange for the forgiveness of souls in purgatory. Medieval Catholicism had reduced a vibrant faith to rituals and obligations, mediated by Church authorities and performed under the threat of corporal punishment.

The conditions for the Reformation included a Catholic Church, the largest landowner in Europe, which was always in dispute with rulers over revenue. Further, European territories were acquiring national identities in Germany, France, Spain, Portugal, and England. Luther owed a debt to the humanism of the Renaissance. Desiderius Erasmus, the sixteenth century priest and Greek scholar, published a Greek translation of the New Testament. In his teachings, he emphasized authentic faith over mechanical religion.

Erasmus determined that the core theological and doctrinal issue with the Reformation was the question of justification and how a sinner finds salvation in Christ. Luther asserted that the doctrine of justification by faith alone is the pinnacle by which the church would stand or fall. The English word justification is derived from the Latin Vulgate (Bible) term *justificare*, which literally means "to make righteous." The

Roman Catholic Church said that justification requires faith and the grace of God, **plus** the works of Jesus Christ. The works of Jesus Christ led to sinners' sanctification before finding salvation in Christ.

Luther and the Protestant Reformers derived their understanding of justification from the Septuagint which is the Greek translation of the Old Testament. Their translation of the English word justification is derived from the Greek word *dikaioo*, which means "to declare righteous." Protestants said that justification is by *sola fide* which means "faith alone." There we have the principle doctrinal difference that sparked one of the most influential religious and cultural changes in the history of the world. Justification was the doctrinal schism that separated the Protestant Reformers and the Catholic Church.

The forces of secular and religious change led to Luther's breakthrough. His pronounced spiritual achievement became that in return for a gospel of grace, the believer would develop a personal relationship with Jesus Christ. The European states endured a long season of religious violence and political absolutism until Luther's vision of human freedom quickened the conscience of western civilization that has endured to this day. It could be said that despite a person's religious beliefs, we are all Protestants now.[51]

During James V's reign, Swiss priest Ulrich Zwingli spread reform, Luther translated the New Testament in German, and John Calvin wrote *Institutes of the Christian Religion*, which explained Protestant beliefs including predestination. In Europe, the Anabaptist movement taught doctrine of baptism only, democratic decision making, and separation of church and state. While in England, parliament passed the Act of Supremacy which made British monarch Henry VIII head of the English church, breaking away from Roman Catholic control.

---

[51] Joseph Loconte, *When Luther Shook Up Christianity*, (The Wall Street Journal).

Unmoved by the expanding political and religious reformation, James continued to strongly support the Catholic Church. On occasion, James defended the faith with horrific, uncivilized violence, such as burning Protestant reformer Patrick Hamilton at the stake in St. Andrews in 1528.

James twice married French women. His first marriage was to Madeleine de Valois, daughter of King Francis of France, who brought with her a large dowry, but of poor health died a few months later. His second marriage was to Mary, daughter of Claude, Duke of Guise. Mary of Guise was born in 1524, and died in 1542. Their children were James and Arthur, both of whom died in infancy, and Mary who descended to become Mary Queen of Scots. James had numerous illegitimate children including James, James (Earl of Moray), Robert (Earl of Orkney), John (Lord Darnley), Adam (Prior of the Perth Charterhouse), Robert (Prior of Whithorn), Jean, and Margaret.

Mary Queen of Scots
(130th Generation)

Mary was Queen of Scotland who ascended to the throne when she was just six days old and coronated as a ten-month-old on September 9, 1543. She ruled for twenty-four years from 1543-1567. She was born on December 8, 1542, at Linlithgow Palace in Scotland, and died on February 8, 1587, when she was executed at Fotheringhay Castle in Northamptonshire, England. The Reformation continued its momentum throughout Europe during Mary's reign despite the Catholic Counter-Reformation in 1545-1563, when the Council of Trent condemned indulgence sellers, immorality of clergy, nepotism, and further denounced Protestantism. In 1549, the Church of England's *Book of Common Prayer* was published to unite most of English churches as a middle ground between Catholicism and Protestantism. It was in 1555, that Queen Mary Tudor of England restored Roman Catholicism to England, banned Protestant translations of the Bible, and persecuted Protestants, leaving many to flee to Geneva, Switzerland, where they printed the Geneva Bible in 1560.

Mary was first promised to Protestant Henry VIII's son Edward, but the union never consummated because of opposition by the Catholic Scottish nobles. At the age of fifteen, on April 24, 1558, she married her first husband, Francis, son of Henry II King of France. Francis became King of France in 1559, but died the following year. Mary returned to Scotland as a Catholic, despite the country officially becoming Protestant following the religious reforms of John Knox. She ruled successfully despite her French styled extravagance that was frowned upon by the Calvinist Scottish nobility.

On July 29, 1565, she married her second cousin, Henry Stewart, Lord Darnley. Much of his character was deplorable and was called vain, conceited, cowardly, weak-minded, and even treacherous. Her turbulent marriage ended when Lord Darnley was found murdered at Kirk O'Field near Edinburgh on February 10, 1567. Although many believe she may have been behind the crime, it is more likely that Lord Darnley died of a disease such as smallpox, following an illness he contracted in Glasgow around Christmas, 1566. Nevertheless, controversy surrounding his death made it very difficult for the monarch to maintain credibility with her subjects, nobles, and foreigners. She was losing their trust and increasingly became isolated. The Queen was at a loss, incapable of coherent thought or independent action, and frequently in tears. She was anguished, sinking into depression, and suffering a near collapse.

Just four months after Darnley's murder, Mary married James Hepburn, Earl of Bothwell, with whom many thought was possibly Lord Darnley's murderer. Mary and Bothwell were married by Protestant rites, something which Mary would later be ashamed of and bitterly regret. This marriage brought conflict again, this time with incurable consequences. The Scottish nobles had lost trust and support for their queen, and imprisoned her in Lochleven Castle where on July 24, 1567, she was forced to renounce the throne to her infant son James VI. After an unsuccessful attempt to regain the throne, she escaped to England where her Protestant cousin, Queen Elizabeth I of England, reluctantly agreed to Mary's execution on February 8, 1587, at Fotheringhay Castle in Northamptonshire, England.

The Protestant Reformation that originated in Germany in 1517, came to Scotland during the reign of Mary. The Reformation in Scotland had political, economic, and religious influences that were tightly interwoven. The political background was the rivalry of French and English interests in Scotland and the struggle between their respective Monarchs. France stood for Catholicism and England was at least anti-papal with some admirable Englishmen and noble enthusiasts. In addition, the Catholic Church in Scotland had too great a share of the national wealth compared to the Crown which was inadequate for its growing obligations.

Mary Queen of Scots was fiercely opposed by an energetic Catholic priest turned Protestant minister, John Knox. The controversial Knox was a noteworthy theologian, writer, and leader of the Reformation. He is considered founder of the Presbyterian Church in Scotland. Knox was an impassioned campaigner for Protestant principles and famously argued with Mary Queen of Scots, a devout Catholic, over Roman beliefs and practices that he believed were idolatrous.

In 1558, while working with John Calvin in Geneva, Switzerland, Knox anonymously wrote and published a pamphlet, *The First Blast of the Trumpet Against the Monstruous Regiment of Women*. "Monstruous" was not quite what it seemed. In Latin, the word means "Rule" and his attack was against the Catholic queens on religious grounds, arguing that rule by females was contrary to the Bible. Excerpts from Knox's *First Blast of the Trumpet* include:

"To promote a woman to bear rule, superiority, dominion, or empire above any realm, nation, or city, is repugnant to nature; an insult to God, a thing most contrary to his revealed will and approved ordinance; and finally, it is the subversion of good order, of all equity and justice;

But now to the second part of nature, in which I include the revealed will and perfect ordinance of God; and against this part of nature, I say, that it does manifestly repugn that any woman shall reign and bear dominion over man. For God, first by the order of his creation, and after by the curse and malediction pronounced against the woman (because of her rebellion) has pronounced the contrary;

And now, to put an end to The First Blast. Seeing that by the order of nature; by the malediction and curse pronounced against woman, by the mouth of St. Paul, the interpreter of God's sentence; by the example of that commonwealth in which God by his word planted order and policy; and, finally, by the judgment of the most godly writers; God has dejected woman from rule, dominion, empire, and authority above man."[52]

Knox led a spiritual and political rebellion against Mary Guise, Dowager Queen of Scotland, Queen Mary I of England, and Mary Queen of Scots. He also published *The Scots Confession*, twenty-five articles that defined correct religious beliefs and practices which was accepted by the Scottish Parliament in 1560. The history of Christianity in Scotland goes back to 400 BC, and the institution itself did not become the established Church of Scotland until 1560, following the Reformation, and the work of John Knox and others.

---

[52] Robert Reed, *The First Blast of the Trumpet Against the Monstrous Regiment of Women*, (Presbyterian Heritage Publications, Dallas, Texas).

Mary was enraged when Knox married his second wife, the staunchly Protestant Margaret Stewart, daughter of Andrew Stewart, second Lord of Ochiltree and a descendant of the Stuart bloodline, as was the Queen herself. She was furious that Knox had dared to marry someone of her own family, the royal house of Stuart, and threatened to drive Knox out of Scotland.

Nevertheless, it was probably a marriage of convenience that eventually produced countless royal bloodline descendants from their three daughters; Martha, Margaret, and Elizabeth. Ironically, Knox's influence and opposition to the crown continued long after his death when his daughter Elizabeth married eminent Church of Scotland minister John Welsh, who was a fierce critic of Mary Queen of Scots' only son, James VI, who became the King of Scotland and England, the first English King of the House of Stuart.[53]

The next three-centuries represent the dawn of modern history and expansion by one of the great sovereign empires to become twenty-five percent of the world's population. During this period, Europeans would migrate to previously unchartered territories in North and South America. More than ten monarchies in Europe will descend from a single British bloodline and the scientific revolution would begin in earnest, changing beliefs about the relationship between God and humankind. The word of God would dramatically expand throughout the world as a result of new printing technology and missionary efforts by religious institutions. This next period is one of the most exciting times ever.

---

[53] Rosalind K. Marshall, *John Knox*, (Birlinn Limited, Edinburgh, Scotland), 187, 215.

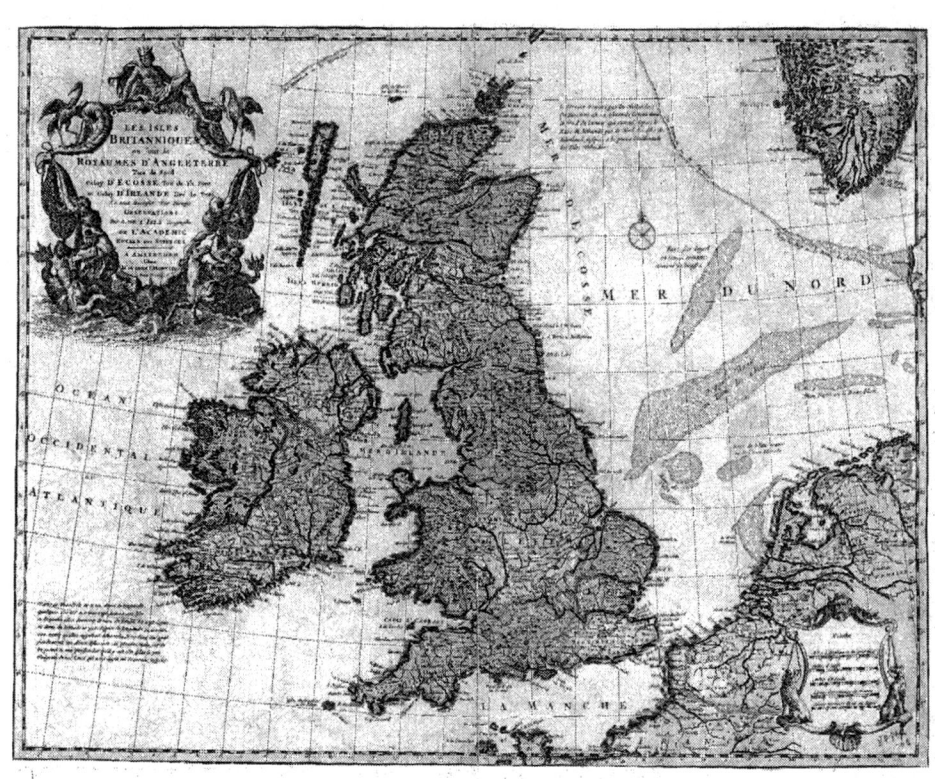

Antique map of the British Isles published at Covensk C. Mortier in
Amsterdam (1700). Courtesy Library of Congress Geography and Maps
Division. This is the region where a boy king ruled sovereign and
united the countries of Scotland and England.

Chapter 12

The Age of United Kingdom (AD 1566)

T he next ten generations extend over a period of three hundred years in what I call The Age of United Kingdom. Unlike many other ages of *The Adam Connection*, this period demonstrates an increasing level of civility, intellectual development, and social justice. At the beginning of this Age, the one-year-old-boy king who would become an intellectual giant, speaking four languages, uniting the countries of Scotland and England, and advancing the supreme authority of the monarchy while decreasing the influence of religious authority. His supremacy was greatly supported by his commissioning scholars to publish a Bible that over time would be printed and read by more than four-hundred-million people. Modern-day scholars consider his Bible as the ancestral language of faith and vocabulary that would underscore early democracy in the United States and throughout western civilization.

This era includes a matrilineal bloodline descendant from whom would spring royal families in ten European countries. The bloodline of this one family under God would traverse to continental Europe and reappear in England as a royal dynasty that continues until modern day. In the eighteenth century of this era, it was the Age of Enlightenment that gave rise to advances in reason, science, and respect for humanity. Some of the most influential thinkers and philosophers of that time originated in the Age of United Kingdom.

Exciting times is an understatement for this ancestral family. The royal bloodline presided over the worldwide expansion of Christian adherents throughout the world including a group of English Protestant reformers who immigrated to the United States in search of a new land and "purified" way of life. This group was known as the Puritans, early pioneers of a fledgling American democracy that evolved to declare and fight for their independence from the British Crown.

All the while, the industrial revolution originated with the invention of the steam engine and transformed a small urban center in Manchester, England, to become a textile giant for the entire world. Transportation and mass production manufacturing would connect people and countries. During this time, the British Empire was at the height of its power and influence, and the world was filled with hope and prosperity. The battles were few and the blessings were many for this ancestral family and people all over the world.

King James VI Scotland / King James I England (131ˢᵗ Generation)

James was born on June 19, 1566, at Edinburgh Castle in Scotland, and died on March 27, 1625, at Theobalds Park in Hertfordshire, England. He ascended to the throne as a one-year-old infant, on July 24, 1567. His coronation was blessed according to the Roman Catholic tradition, by the energetic reformer, Bishop of Orkney; and John Knox preached the sermon during the ceremony in the Church of the Holy Rude in Stirling, Scotland.

So it was that James VI became King of Scotland from 1567 and united the kingdom as James I, King of England from 1603. As successor to Queen Elizabeth I in England, he was unpopular with Puritans because of his traditional theological views and ritualistic practices. He was generally unpopular with Parliament because of his extravagant lifestyle and schemes to politically align with Spain.

His religious policy involved assertion of the supreme authority of the monarchy and suppression of both Puritans and Catholics who opposed his policy. The preparation of the Authorized Version of the Bible in English was ordered by James and published in 1611. Famously, James thwarted Guy Fawkes and his anti-Catholic plot to blow up Parliament in 1605.

His childhood was miserable, harsh, and often frightening. His father was dead, his mother a prisoner in England, in effect, he was an orphan. His tutor was the scholar, George Buchanan, one of the most profound intellectuals in sixteenth century Scotland. In one respect, Buchanan did his work well. James was taught Latin before he could write English, and the young king learned his lessons thoroughly, becoming a notable scholar himself. The adolescent monarch also learned Greek, and as an adult would be able to converse in French, Italian, and Spanish. A harsh taskmaster and partisan, Buchanan taught James that his mother was a wicked woman and an adulteress guilty of his father's murder. It would be years before James could free his mind of the poisonous version of his family tragedy and break out of his timid, lonely, loveless childhood.[54]

While his political accomplishments were many and his social practices at times were flamboyant and merry, James changed the world by

---

[54] Allan Massie, *The Royal Stuarts*, (Thomas Dunne Books, New York, NY), 147.

his religious beliefs, beginning in 1604. He commissioned fifty-four Church of England scholars to collaborate, create, and publish, what would become in 1611, the King James Bible. The scholars used the Bishops Bible (1568 Church of England translation) and Tyndale's Bible (1526) as well as available Greek and Hebrew manuscripts.

It's barely possible to overstate the significance of this Bible. With an estimated four-hundred-million copies published, the King James Bible became the most widely read literature in the history of the world. For the next 300 years and ten generations, it became the most popular translation of the Holy Bible. At its publishing, the King James Bible found a critical balance in a world of theological conflict, and it has been beloved since then by every denomination of Protestant churches and congregations. By the end of the seventeenth century it was simply the Bible.

While it has only recently been superseded by translations in more modern English, these modern translations are based on sources that the King James translators couldn't have known in their time. To Christians all around the world, it is still the ancestral language of faith. To modern readers, the English of the King James Bible sounds archaic, much as Shakespeare does. But there would have been an archaism for readers even in 1611 because the King James Bible draws heavily from a version of William Tyndale's New Testament published in 1534 and from translations by Miles Coverdale also published in the 1530s. Tyndale's aspiration was to make his New Testament accessible to the masses. Though readers often talk about the majesty of the King James Bible, what has made it live is in fact the simplicity of its language. Scholars have often debated just how much the King James Bible has influenced the English language. The King James Bible has had an enormous impact on English for the very reason that it captures, preserves, and communicates down through the centuries the unavoidable rhythms of good English.[55]

More so, the King James Bible impacted the English-speaking world in unparalleled ways. It has carried the Protestant faith and word of God around the world. The King James Bible was a foundation for the will and belief that forged America and other British colonies. Known in America as the King James Version, this Bible provided the vocabulary, seedbed, and construction model for the early development of democracy. Enforcers of slavery used The King James Version Bible as did the liberators of slavery and the slaves themselves embraced this Bible as a liberation theology. The King James and King James Version Bibles have inspired global missionaries and provided hope for the hopeless. It became the inspiration for gospel music and spirituals that set into motion soul, blues, jazz, and rock. Abraham Lincoln said, "It is the best book that God has given to man." "It is impossible to rightly govern the world without God and the Bible," said George Washington, founding President of the United States.

Reformed church institutions that integrated the King James Version Bible in their theology were founders of some of the greatest universities in world history including Harvard, Princeton, and Yale. The majority of those people who formed the Royal Society, a scientific academy for the UK and Commonwealth, were hard-reading Bible men. The intellectual energy, social acceptance, and moral authority that science gained through its close association with the King James Bible undoubtedly benefited scientists such as Descartes, Galileo, and Newton. It can be said that the King James Bible in the early seventeenth century joined together religion and science in a marriage that has held despite and because of enlightenment.

---

[55] Verlyn Klinkenborg, *The King James Bible At 400*, (New York Times).

New English words and phrases that have flourished since publication of the King James Bible include, "Let there be light," "fell flat on his face," "let my people go," "the apple of his eye," "a man after his own heart," "sign of the times," "ye of little faith," "the meek shall inherit the earth, "under the sun," "to rise and shine," "the land of the living," "sour grapes," "from time to time," and hundreds more that are indelibly written in the hearts and minds of people of all religious and secular beliefs in Western civilization.

During his memorable monarchy, on November 21, 1589, at the age of twenty-three, James married Anne, daughter of King Frederick II of Denmark. They had three daughters, Margaret, Mary, and Sophia all of whom died as infants. Their other children were Henry (Prince of Wales), Charles (his successor as King of England), Robert (Duke of Kintyre), and Elizabeth who married Frederick V, Count Palatine of the Rhine and King of Bohemia.

Elizabeth Stuart
(132nd Generation)

Elizabeth Stuart was born at Falkland Palace in Fife, Scotland, on August 19, 1596, and died of Pneumonia on February 13, 1662. She was the wife of Frederick V, and became Electress Palantine and briefly Queen of Bohemia. She was the second child, eldest daughter of James VI, and four years older than her brother Charles who became the last King of England with the Stuart dynasty. Most other European royal families, including those of Belgium, Denmark, Luxemburg, Netherlands, Norway, and Sweden, as well as formerly of Germany, Greece, Romania, and Russia are descendants of Elizabeth Stuart. Elizabeth spoke several languages including French, was extremely literate, and had a thorough understanding of the Protestant religion. She and her husband Frederick shared a common ancestor in Henry II of England.

There were many religious developments during this era, including separatists rejecting the Church of England and sailing to America on the Mayflower. Some years later, with a desire to cleanse the Church of England, Puritans emigrated and started the colonies in what became the United States of America. In 1642, the Italian scientist, astronomer, physicist, mathematician, inventor, and philosopher, Galileo Galilei died with his discoveries disputed and censured by the Catholic Church in Rome.

It was in 1632 that Galileo angered the Pope when he published a book in which he openly stated that the Earth was moving around the Sun, in contrast to established Church doctrine at the time. After being imprisoned and later confined to his home in Florence, Italy, Galileo put forward his concept of "Basic Relativity" in Physics, which later formed the basis for Einstein's Special Theory of Relativity.

In 1646, the Westminster Confession was accepted as the statement of Presbyterianism in Scotland and England. The Quaker movement led by preacher George Fox was founded the next year and in 1648, the Thirty Years War ended, upon which Catholics and Protestants were given equal rights in most of the Holy Roman Empire.

Elizabeth and Frederick had eight daughters and five sons including Henry (King of Bohemia), Charles Lewis (Count Palatine of the Rhine), Rupert (Count Palatine of the Rhine), Edward (Count Palatine of the Rhine), Maurice (Count Palatine of the Rhine), Edward (Count Palatine of the Rhine and Duke of Nevers), and Sophia (Heiress Presumptive of England and Consort of Hannover).

Sophia
(133rd Generation)

Sophia was born on October 14, 1630, in The Hague, Netherlands and died on June 8, 1714, in Hanover, Germany. She was Electress of Hannover from 1692-1698 and became heir presumptive to the crowns of England and Ireland under the Act of Settlement in 1701 which was legislation that ensured a Protestant line of succession and opposed the claim of the Catholic Prince James Edward Stuart, the son of King James I. After the Act of Union that unified England and Scotland in 1707, she became heir presumptive to the throne of the Kingdom of Great Britain.

Sophia grew up in the Netherlands, where her family fled for safety during the Thirty Years' War (1618-1648) in Europe. This series of wars involved sixteen European states and the Emperor of Rome who were at issue over religious, dynastic, territorial, and commercial interests. Its destructive campaigns and battles resulted in over eight million casualties and ended in 1648, with the Treaty of Westphalia in Germany. The balance of power in Europe forever changed with France becoming a chief Western power, Netherlands recognized as an independent republic, and Sweden controlling the Baltic region. The ancient notion of a Roman Catholic empire headed spiritually by a pope was abandoned forever and modern Europe was established as a community of sovereign states.

On September 30, 1658, Sophia married Ernest Augustus (Duke of Brunswick and Luneburg, Duke of Hannover, Elector of Hannover), a second cousin of Sophia's mother Elizabeth Stuart. Sophia and Ernest were both great-grandchildren of Christian II of Denmark. Their children were George Lewis (King of England), Frederick Augustus, Maximillan William (Imperial Field Marshall), Charles Philip,

Christian, Ernest Augustus (Duke of York and Albany), and Sophia Charlotte (Queen of Prussia).

King George I
(134th Generation)

George, King of Great Britain, reigned for twelve years from 1714-1727. He was born on May 28, 1660, in Hanover, Germany, and died of a stroke on June 11, 1727, in Hannover, Germany. He married his cousin Sophia Dorothea of Celle (Germany) in 1682, and in addition to his three illegitimate children, together they had two children, Sophia (Queen of Prussia and mother of Frederick the Great) and George Agustus (Prince of Wales, afterwards her successor King of Great Britain). Their marriage was unhappy and marred by infidelity.

George was the first monarch of the House of Guelph, a European dynasty that has included many German and British monarchs from the eleventh to the twenty-first century. While George was fluent in German and French and conversational in Latin, Italian, and Dutch, he had limited capacity in the spoken and written English language. His treatment of his wife Sophia was viewed as scandalous by his British subjects. During George's reign, he was constantly ridiculed and the monarchy began to diminish in power as Britain began to transition to a cabinet-style government led by a Prime Minister.

King George II
(135th Generation)

King George II, christened as George Augustus, was born on October 30, 1683, in Hanover, Germany, and died of an Aneurysm on October 25, 1760, at Kensington Palace in London, England. He reigned for thirty-three years from 1727-1760. He married Wilhelmina Charlotte Caroline, daughter of Margrave of Bradenburg and together they had four sons and five daughters. They were George William Frederick (Prince of Wales and afterwards King George III), Edward Augustus (Duke of York and Albany, Earl of Ulster), William Henry (Duke of Gloucester and Edinburg, Earl of Connaught), Henry Frederick (Duke of Cumberland and Strathearn, Earl of Dublin), Frederick William, Augusta (Duchess of Bruswick-Wolfenbuttel), Elizabeth Caroline, Louisa Ann, and Caroline Matilda.

Frederick
(136ᵗʰ Generation)

Frederick Louis, Prince of Wales, was born in Hanover, Germany on February 1, 1707, and died from a likely pulmonary embolism in Taplow, England, on March 31, 1751. In his youth, Frederick was a spendthrift and womanizer. An unpopular prince known for sports gambling, Fredrick became a patron of the arts later in life. He was the tenth Chancellor of the University of Dublin from 1728-1751, and a portrait of him still prominently displays in the Hall of the Trinity College, Dublin.

In 1735, he married sixteen-year-old Augusta of Saxe-Gotha-Altenberg who was born on November 30, 1719. Frederick became a devoted family man and lived with his wife and children in the countryside at Cliveden. Augusta was Princess of Wales from 1736 to1756, and Dowager Princess of Wales thereafter upon the death of her husband Frederick.

After Frederick's death and following the last nine years of George II's reign, Augusta's eldest son succeeded his grandfather (George II) as George III in 1760. Augusta died of throat cancer on February 8, 1772.

Frederick's and Augusta's children were Agusta (Duchess of Brunswick), George III (future King of Great Britain), Edward (Duke of York), Elizabeth, William Henry (Duke of Gloucester), Henry (Duke of Cumberland), Louisa, Frederick, and Caroline Matilda (Queen of Denmark and Norway).

King George III
(137th Generation)

George William Frederick was King of United Kingdom of Great Britain and Ireland who reigned for fifty-nine years from 1761-1820. He was born on June 4, 1738, in London, England, and died on January 29, 1820, in Windsor, England. During his life, George suffered from a rare hereditary disease called porphyria, that caused paralysis, deliriousness, hypertension, and acute pain that ultimately led to complications that ended his life. He was crowned on September 22, 1761, at Westminster Abbey in London, England. He married Sophia Charlotte of Mecklenburg-Strelitz (Germany) whom he met for the first time on their wedding day. They had a happy marriage and produced fifteen children.

In 1762, King George III purchased Buckingham House in London which later become Buckingham Palace, the official residence of the monarch when in London. George was a God-fearing moral man, well educated in science and the arts, and had a special interest in agricultural development. The spinning frame and steam engine were invented during his reign. Also during his reign, George transferred to Parliament the right of income from Crown Estates in return for a Civil List annuity for his domestic upkeep and expenses, an arrangement that has continued until the present day.

During his tumultuous reign, his Prime Minister levied a tax and high customs duties on every official document in the British colonies, except for a tax on tea. That was until the Tea Act of May 10, 1773, whereby the American colonists famously revolted against the new tax, and threw tea chests overboard in the Boston Harbor in what became known as the "Boston Tea Party." The American War of Independence followed beginning in April 1775, and was officially declared by the U.S. Continental Congress on July 4, 1776. Britain agreed to recognize American independence in the Treaty of Paris on September 3, 1783.

Upon facing the political and military realities of his now diminished empire, George suffered mental incapacities which plagued him for the rest of his life, so much so, that his son George, Prince of Wales, was made permanent regent in 1810. Other seminal events during his monarchy included The Act of Union with Ireland in 1800 which united the Parliaments of England and Ireland, The War of 1812, and the defeat of Napoleon Bonaparte at Waterloo in 1815, marking the end of the Napoleonic wars. Notably in 1781, Immanuel Kant published his *Critique of Pure Reason*, considered one of the most influential works in the history of philosophy. A brief excerpt from the *Critique* states, "Reason cannot deny the existence of God, the soul or eternity."

George and Sophia's children were George Augustus Frederick (Prince of Wales and later King George IV), Frederick Augustus (Duke of York and Albany, Prince and Bishop of Osnaburg), William Henry (Duke of Clarence and afterwards King George V), Edward Augustus, Duke of Kent and Strathearn, Earl of Dublin), Ernest Augustus (Duke of Brunswick-Luneburg and King of Hannover), Augustus Frederick (Duke of Sussex, Earl of Inverness and Baron Arklow), Adolophus Frederick (first Duke of Cambridge, Earl of Tipperary and Baron Culloden), Octavius, Alfred, Charlotte Augusta Matilda (Princess Royal), Augusta Sophia, Elizabeth, Mary, Sophia, and Amelia.

Edward
(138ᵗʰ Generation)

Prince Edward was Duke of Kent and Strathearn who was born on November 2, 1767, and died on January 23, 1820. He was the fourth son and fifth child of King George III and father of Queen Victoria.

During his era in 1807, William Wilberforce, a member of Parliament and devout Christian, led Parliament to permanently abolish the slave trade in the British Empire. Wilberforce and other Christians also addressed pressing social problems including exploitative child labor, illiteracy, education prison reform, and reinstating the civil rights of Jews and Catholics.

Edward was the first member of the royal family to live in North America and credited with first using the term "Canadian" meaning both French and English settlers in Canada. After a distinguished military career, Edward was promoted in May 1799, to the rank of general and appointed Commander in Chief of British forces in North America.

At the age of fifty, on May 29, 1818, Edward married the widow, Princess Victoria of Saxe-Coburg-Saalfeld in Germany, daughter of Duke Franz Friedrich and together they had one child, Princess Alexandrina Victoria of Kent who became Queen Victoria.

Queen Victoria
(139ᵗʰ Generation)

Alexandria Victoria, known as Victoria, was Queen of the United Kingdom of Great Britain and Ireland who reigned for sixty-three years from June 20, 1837, until her death. She was born on May 24, 1819, at Kensington Palace in London, England, and died on January 22, 1901, at Osborne, Isle of Wight. In February 1840, Victoria married her cousin, Albert Ernest Albert of Saxe-Coburg and Gotha. Albert was born on August 26, 1819, in Coburg, in the Duchy of Saxe-Coburg and Gotha in Germany and died on December 14, 1861, at Windsor Castle, United Kingdom.

Queen Victoria had majestic strength of character and conducted State business in a manner that put beyond all reason of doubt her fitness as a woman to rule. During her monarchy, the British Empire was at the height of its power and she reigned over four-hundred-fifty million people, one-quarter of the world's population and approximately one-quarter of the world's landmass, stretching from Canada to the Caribbean, Africa, India, Australia, and New Zealand.

The Victorian era was one of the most exciting times in the history of Great Britain with the onset of the industrial revolution, as well as political, trade, scientific, and military developments. Noteworthy events during her rule included the launch of the world's first all metal ship, the construction of railways in Britain, signaling of the first trans-Atlantic telegraph service, publication of Charles Darwin's *The Origin of the Species*, the building the world's first underground railway in London, the founding of The Salvation Army and The Football Association, the legalization of trade unions, the founding of the Labor Party, and establishment of mandatory, compulsory, free schooling for children.

Victoria and Albert's children were Albert Edward (Prince of Wales and afterwards King Edward VII), Albert Ernest Albert (Duke of Saxe-Coburg and Gotha), Arthur William Patrick (first Duke of Connaught and Strathearn and Earl of Sussex), Leopold George Duncan Albert (first Duke of Albany, Earl of Clarence, and Baron of Arklow), Victoria Adelaide Mary Louisa (Princess Royal), Alice Maud Mary (Duchess of Hessee), Helena Augusta Victoria, and Beatrice Mary Victoria.

King Edward VII (140ᵗʰ Generation)

Albert Edward was King of The United Kingdom of Great Britain and Ireland and reigned for nine years from January 22, 1901, until his death. He was born on November 9, 1841, at Buckingham Palace in London, England, and died on May 6, 1910, at Buckingham Palace. He married Alexandra, daughter of King Christian IX of Denmark, on March 10, 1863, at St. George's Chapel in Windsor Castle. She was born December 1, 1844, in Copenhagen, Denmark, and died on November 20, 1925, at Sandringham House in Norfolk, England.

Despite high times for the social elite in Europe, society was changing during the Edwardian period as socialism, women suffragettes, the Labor party, and trade unions were gaining stature, and these founding movements led to the development of Britain's social welfare system. Edward was likeable and outgoing, but became known as a philanderer interested in eating, drinking, and other men's wives.

Alexandra tolerated Edward's succession of mistresses who included Lady Churchill (mother of Winston Churchill) and Alice Keppel (great-grandmother of Camilla wife of Charles who would become Edward's great-great-grandson, future Prince of Wales, and heir apparent to the throne).

During Edward's era, science and religion was shaken to its core when in 1859, Charles Darwin published *Origin of the Species*, against a backdrop of Christianity spreading vigorously in Africa and Hong Kong, and more than three-hundred-thousand Armenian Christians massacred by the Turks. The U.S. Civil War had ended and notably, the Salvation Army was founded in London's East End by one-time Methodist minister William Booth and his wife Catherine. Today, the Salvation Army has worldwide membership of more than 1.5 million members.

Albert and Alexandra's children were Albert Victor Christian Edward (Duke of Clarence and Avondale, Earl of Athlone), George Frederick Ernest Albert (Prince of Wales and later King George V), Alexander John Charles Albert, Louise Victoria Alexandra Dagmar (Princess Royal), Victoria Alexandra Olga Mary, and Maud Charlotte Olga Mary (Princess and Queen of Norway).

The next short six decades represent one of the longest periods of human tragedy, carnage, and casualties. This time in human history is best characterized by madness and mayhem. Historians will note these next three generations as a world at war. The shame of this next age will be dominated by unspeakable acts of murder by a totalitarian, anti-Semitic regime with a hellish belief in their racial supremacy.

Antique map of Europe (1760). During the Great War and World War II, virtually every country was invaded by Nazi Germany, Italy, or the Soviet Union. During this period, the British monarchs demonstrated resolve and perseverance in the face of unthinkable loss of life and re-order of the British Empire and social structures in the world.

Chapter 13

The Age of World Wars (AD 1865)

The next three generations and sixty-one years was one of the most devastating periods in human history. This Age of World Wars is seemingly unequaled in atrocities committed against humanity. When I look back over *The Adam Connection* ancestral story, it's difficult to compare murders and mayhem of ancient times compared to this era. The senseless violence in previous generations is perhaps easier to understand given what might be considered uncivilized periods in history. However, in this Age of World Wars, civilized nations took advantage of their industrial power to wreak havoc on other nations and their people. Sixteen-million lives were lost in the Great War, and sixty-million lives were lost in the Second World War. If considering this horrific loss of life is not mind-numbing enough, we also know that some six-million lives were lost from ethnic cleansing and genocide. The times were unimaginable.

The first king in this era oversaw the downfall of great European empires and rise of social and economic systems that repressed people and empowered dictatorial political leaders. The British Empire was also facing fractures in their commonwealth of nations as countries sought home rule and independence. One can only imagine the effect on history if this king were not a man of peace and loyalist during a world at war. He was a family man and simple Christian who was committed to God, his nation, and his family.

It was the last king of The Age of World Wars who distinguished himself and his country by working so tirelessly with his government to push back the tides of tyranny emanating from Europe and Asia. By all accounts, the royal couple rose to the occasion in helping the country deal with the hardships of a world at war. With the real threat of invasion by bellicose nations, this king of steady resolve, overcame his speech impediment and courageously spoke with his country by radio, with calm and certainty of God's blessing on the United Kingdom. At the end of his reign, his country entered a period of austerity, and the British Empire transformed into a Commonwealth of independent nations.

Excerpts from *A Tale of Two Cities (1859)* by Charles Dickens perfectly summarize The Age of World Wars; "it was the worst of times, it was the age of foolishness, it was the epoch of incredulity, it was the season of Darkness, it was the winter of despair, we had nothing before us, were all going the other way (from heaven)."

King George V
(141st Generation)

George Frederick Ernest Albert, became the first British monarch from the newly styled House of Windsor. He became King George V of the United Kingdom of Great Britain and Ireland, who ascended to the throne on May 6, 1910, and ruled for twenty-five years until his death. He was born on June 3, 1865, at Marlborough House in London, England, and died on January 20, 1936, at Sandringham in Norfolk, England. As Prince George, he married Princess Victoria Mary of Teck in London on July 6, 1893, at the Chapel Royal, in St James's Palace. Victoria Mary was known as Mary or by her family as "May." They became Duke and Duchess of York and lived on the Sandringham Estate, until his ascension. Mary was born on May 26, 1867, at Kensington Palace, London, and died on March 24, 1953, at Marlborough House, London.

As a young man, Prince George served in the Royal Navy for fifteen years. His postings abroad led him to China, South Africa, West Indies, Australia, Japan, and South America. During these formative years, he developed a keen sense of patriotism and enhanced his belief in the idea of the British Empire. He was a beloved King who enjoyed stamp collecting and in 1932, he instigated the tradition of the Royal Christmas radio broadcast to the nation and commonwealth, a tradition that continues to present day.

His reign was one of unrelenting restlessness, overseeing the downfall of the great empires of Russia, Germany, and Austro-Hungary and rise of socialism, communism, and fascism. He was enmeshed in demands for Irish Home Rule and Indian self-government. An ingrained conservative, indifferent to science, politics, history, and the arts, this King and man of peace was a robust wartime loyalist. His idyllic marriage to Mary protected and sustained him in his lonely task as a world-at-war monarch. He was a simple, uncomplicated Christian who had habits of devotion that sustained him throughout his life.

The Accession Council met at St. James Palace to formally declare the accession of King George V and the new monarch swore his loyalty to Parliament and the Church of England. The Accession Council made a 'Proclamation of Accession' from when George V ascended to the throne:

"WHEREAS it has pleased Almighty God to call to His Mercy our late Sovereign Lord King Edward the Seventh of Blessed and Glorious memory, by whose Decease the Crown is solely and rightfully come to the High and Mighty Prince George Frederick Ernest Albert:

WE, therefore, the Lords Spiritual and Temporal of this Realm, being here assisted with these of His late Majesty's Privy Council, with numbers of other Principal Gentlemen of Quality, with the Lord Mayor, Aldermen, and Citizens of London, do now hereby with one voice and Consent of Tongue and Heart publish and proclaim:

That the High and Mighty Prince George Frederick Ernest Albert is now, by the death of our late Sovereign of happy memory, become our only lawful and rightful, liege Lord George the Fifth, by the Grace of God, King of the United Kingdom of Great Britain and Ireland, and of the British Dominions beyond the seas, Defender of the Faith, Emperor of India; to whom we do acknowledge all Faith and constant Obedience, with hearty and humble Affection, beseeching God, by whom Kings and Queens do reign, to bless the Royal Prince George the Fifth, with long and happy Years to reign over us.[56]

The foreshadowing moment that defined George's monarchy was when Britain entered the First World War (World War I) on August 12, 1914. This Great War was a global war originating in Europe that lasted from July 28, 1914 to November 11, 1918. The war principally involved the world's great economic powers in two opposing alliances, Allies involving France, Russia, and the United Kingdom of Great Britain, and Ireland versus the Central European powers of Germany and Austria-Hungary. These alliances were expanded as more nations entered the war: Italy, Japan, and the United States joined the Allies, while the Ottoman Empire (Turkey) and Bulgaria joined the Central Powers.

One of the bloodiest conflicts in human history, the Great War claimed over nine million military and seven million civilian lives. The Austro-Hungarian Empire agreed to an armistice with the Allies on November 4, 1918, as did Germany at 11 A.M. on November 11, 1918, thereby, ending a state of war between Germany and the Allied Powers,

---

[56] Kenneth Rose, *King George V*, (Phoenix Press, London, England), xii, 4, 75.

consisting mainly The United Kingdom, United States, France, Italy, and Japan. Formal peace was memorialized at The Treaty of Versailles on June 28, 1919. By the end of the war, the German Empire, Russian Empire, Austro-Hungarian Empire, and the Ottoman Empire ceased to exist and national borders were redrawn.

In 1917, due to the anti-German sentiment from World War I, King George changed his family name from Saxe-Coburg-Gotha (commonly known as Brunswick or Hanover) to Windsor, and relinquished all his German titles and family connections.

With George's change of his family name, he became the patriarch of The House of Windsor, a royal house of the United Kingdom and other Commonwealth dominions. The Windsor dynasty is of German paternal descent which succeeded the House of Hanover and from which subsequent kings and queens of The United Kingdom of Great Britain and Ireland will descend.

As was accustomed by the Victorian upper classes, George and Mary raised their children out of the public view, employing a hierarchy of nannies and nursery maids, governesses and tutors to relieve themselves from the day-to-day duties of child rearing. Their children were Edward Albert Christian George Andrew Patrick David (afterwards King Edward III and later Duke of Windsor), Albert Frederick Arthur George (afterwards King George VI), Henry William Frederick Albert (Duke of Gloucester), George Edward Alexander Edmund (Duke of Kent), John Charles Francis, and Victoria Alexandria Alice Mary (The Princess Royal).

King Edward VIII
(142nd Generation)

Edward was the second British monarch from the House of Windsor who ascended to the throne on January 20, 1936, but was never crowned.

He was born on June 23, 1894, at White Lodge in Richmond, England, and died in Paris on May 28, 1972. He married an American, Wallis Simpson and they had no children. He reigned for ten months and twenty-one days and abdicated the throne on December 11, 1936.

Edward was a popular Prince of Wales who served in the Army during World War I, but was forbidden to go to the front line. His relationship with his parents was quite strained due to his liaisons with married women and his carefree social behavior.

After becoming King, Edward created a constitutional crisis resulting from his desire to marry Wallis Simpson as she was a divorcee and still married to her second husband. By all accounts, she was pursuing the King because of his wealth and position, and it was felt that she would be an unsuitable queen. On December 11, 1936, Edward abdicated the throne and left for France, where the couple were married on June 3, 1937, at the Château de Candé near Tours, France. Edward and Wallis would then become The Duke and Duchess of Windsor, though they were disliked and distanced by his family who felt he had let the family and country down because he had not done his duty. His brother George ascended to the crown upon Edward's abdication.

King George VI
(143rd Generation)

Albert Frederick Arthur George, was the third British monarch from the House of Windsor who as King George VI of the United Kingdom, reigned for fifteen years from December 11, 1936, until his death. He was born on December 14, 1895, at Sandringham, in Norfolk, England, and died on February 6, 1952, at Sandringham. The twenty-eight-year-old Prince Albert, married Lady Elizabeth Angela Marguerite Bowes-Lyon on April 26, 1923, at Westminster Abbey in

London, England. Genealogists have managed to prove that Elizabeth and George were both descended from King Robert I of Scotland.

Elizabeth was born on August 4, 1900, at the stately home in St. Paul's Walden Bury in England, and died at the age of 101 on March 30, 2002, at Royal Lodge in Windsor, England. She was a vibrant, attractive woman who was the youngest of ten children of the fourteenth Earl of Strathmore and grew up in a very united, loving, self-confident, and largely unpretentious family. The Strathmores were a devoutly religious family who prayed every day in the little chapel at their country estate. Upright, open, and straightforward, this family flock lived by a simple, upper-class code, which made them at once fun-loving and considerate.

Undermined and scorned by his oppressive father George V, and distanced by his cold and somewhat unloving mother, Queen Mary, the young Prince Albert profoundly lacked self-confidence that caused him to stammer badly in public and at times became incoherent, inarticulate, and unpredictable in his social behavior.[57]

Fortified by the immense influence of his Queen, the King swiftly gained popularity in his own right given his honesty, goodness, and how he handled the aftermath of the abdication in a manner that restored confidence in the monarchy.

However, the reign of George VI was overwhelmingly defined by Britain's defense against the monstrous Nazi regime and the unimaginable loss of human life during the Second World War (World War II). From September 1, 1939, and the six years that followed, an estimated sixty-million people died during this war. Included in this loss of life, was the atrocious genocide of six-million Jews during The Holocaust, including an estimated one-million-five-hundred-thousand children. World War II was a global war that involved most of the world's nations,

---

[57] Denis Judd, *George VI*, (I.B. Tauris & Co Ltd., London, England), xiii, 57, 179.

including the great economic, industrial, and scientific powers forming two alliances: The Allies and the Axis. The Allies were led by Great Britain, United States, and Russia while the Axis nations included Germany, Italy, and Japan. Appallingly, World War II was the deadliest conflict in human history.

It must be said with great admiration that the royal couple rose to the occasion of helping their country grapple with the horrors of World War II. George and his prime minister, Winston Churchill, developed a close personal working relationship and met regularly to discuss the progress of the War. George VI's bearing during the Second World War, and particularly during the first two years of the conflict when it seemed that Britain might at any moment be invaded and overwhelmed, confirmed his reputation as a monarch of supreme integrity and courage, a people's king. George VI did not falter. The united resolve of King and Prime Minister prevented a wholescale flee to safety in the English countryside by the Crown's Court, Government, and Parliament. Such plans for dispersal of the political and ruling elite had been made by the previous Government until George VI and Churchill tore the plans up. The King and Queen steadfastly remained in London throughout the German blitzkrieg, showing love and care for their people.[58]

World War II transformed the political alliances and social structures of the world. During his post-World War II reign, the United Nations was established to foster international co-operation and prevent future conflicts, the United States and Soviet Union emerged as rival superpowers, and Europe's influence and power diminished resulting in the beginning of decolonization of Asia and Africa. Following the War, Britain entered a period of economic austerity and the British Empire

---

[58] Denis Judd, Ibid, 179.

began to be replaced by the Commonwealth of Nations as former colonies became independent, most notably, India.

King George and Elizabeth's children are Elizabeth Alexandra Mary (afterwards Queen Elizabeth II) and Margaret Rose.

The next and final generation in this story that connects Adam to Modern age humanity, is one of hope and possibilities. A young princess ascends to the British throne and would rule in tumultuous times with style and grace. Duty, honor, and courage are embodied in this Christian sovereign ruler. She is a woman who lives her faith in a world that changes at the speed of technology. This descendant of Adam can surely be called a child of God.

Antique map of the British Empire throughout the World (circa 1850).
Courtesy Library of Congress Geography and Maps Division. With the
British Empire in decline, the commonwealth of nations will maintain
traditions with new found independence. The reigning monarch in this age,
will lead with charm, grace, and Christian moral values.

Chapter 14

The Age of World
Possibilities (AD 1926)

———————————————

The next generation is the last one in this story. This is The Age of World Possibilities. Following an era when the world was at war for ten years and more than seventy-six million lives were lost, we enter a time of both eternal hope and continued conflict between people and nations. The dawn of this era is the birth of a child, who upon her coronation at the age of twenty-seven, would become the longest serving monarch in world history.

There is much to be admired about this once-in-a-generation queen. Growing up in war-torn London, this princess learned how to drive and maintain a commercial truck. She is by all accounts a modern-day leader who understands the world. Words like grace, humility, and duty describe the bearing and substance of this monarch. The Queen in this Age of World Possibilities understands her role and responsibilities toward the British people, government, Church of England, and Commonwealth. As the Head of the fifty-four-member Commonwealth of Nations, this Queen has leadership responsibilities for a group of nations and people who share a common language and promote good government, economic development, and human rights. She and her family support thousands of public and private charities that provide social benefit for people and communities of interest. During her reign, she has visited over one-hundred countries to support the interests of her United Kingdom and Commonwealth of Nations.

The Queen of this Age of World Possibilities is a devout Christian who gracefully conducts her life and performs her work based on moral values learned from her family, the Anglican Church, and personal relationship with Jesus Christ. Her gift is one of influencing without control. She has a high-standard of service and commitment to God and her country.

During this Age of World Possibilities, the reign of this Queen is not defined by the regional conflicts in the Middle East and Asia. It is not defined by the technological advances derived from computers and communication technologies. The scientific advances of this era do not define her reign. It is her goodness and commitment to God that defines her reign. One of her Christmas messages summarized her belief that God sent Jesus Christ to be the Savior of the world with the power to forgive. His forgiveness can heal families, restore relationships, and reconcile divided communities. She is the last descendant of this one family under God that provides tangible evidence that we are all connected.

Queen Elizabeth II
(144th Generation)

Elizabeth Alexandra Mary is the fourth monarch of the House of Windsor who became Queen Elizabeth II of the United Kingdom of Great Britain and Ireland. She ascended to the throne on February 6, 1952, and on September 10, 2015, Queen Elizabeth II became the longest ever reigning British monarch surpassing the sixty-three years seven months reigned by her great-great-grandmother Queen Victoria.

Princess Elizabeth was born on April 21, 1926, at 17 Bruton Street in London, England, and on November 20, 1947, she married Prince Philip Mountbatten. Philip is the son of Prince Andrew of Greece and Denmark and Princess Alice of Battenberg. Elizabeth and Philip are second cousins once removed through King Christian IX of Denmark and third cousins from Queen Victoria. The children of Elizabeth and Philip are Charles, Philip Arthur George (Prince of Wales), Andrew Albert Christian Edward (Duke of York), Edward Antony Richard Louis (Earl of Wessex), and Anne Elizabeth Alice Louise (Princess Royal).

As customary since 1415, the Accession Council met at St. James Palace to formally declare the accession of Queen Elizabeth II and the new monarch swore in return her loyalty to Parliament and the Church of England. The Accession Council made a "Proclamation of Accession" from when Elizabeth II ascended to the throne:

"WHEREAS it has pleased Almighty God to call to His Mercy our late Sovereign Lord King George the Sixth of Blessed and Glorious memory, by whose Decease the Crown is solely and rightfully come to the High and Mighty Princess Elizabeth Alexandra Mary:

WE, therefore, the Lords Spiritual and Temporal of this Realm, being here assisted with these His late Majesty's Privy Council, with representatives of other Members of the Commonwealth, with other Principal Gentlemen of Quality, with the Lord Mayor, Aldermen, and Citizens of London, do now hereby with one voice and Consent of Tongue and Heart publish and proclaim that the High and Mighty Princess Elizabeth Alexandra Mary is now, by the death of our late Sovereign of happy memory, become Queen Elizabeth the Second, by the Grace of God Queen of this Realm and of all Her other Realms and Territories, Head of the Commonwealth, Defender of the Faith, to whom Her lieges do acknowledge all Faith and constant Obedience with hearty and humble

Affection, beseeching God by whom Kings and Queens do reign, to bless the Royal Princess Elizabeth the Second with long and happy Years to reign over us.

Given at St. James's Palace this Sixth Day of February in the year of our Lord one thousand nine hundred and fifty-two."

Before she had ascended to the throne, Princess Elizabeth became a state counselor on her eighteenth birthday and served in the Auxiliary Territorial Service during World War II. In doing so, she learned to drive a three-ton truck in congested London traffic, change wheels and spark-plugs, understand the workings of ignition systems, bleed brakes, and dismantle and build engines. This thoroughly modern servant leader understands the world in which she lives.

Throughout Britain's changing position in the world and trans-forming social and economic structures, Queen Elizabeth has con-ducted her office with humility, grace, and duty in a manner that has endeared herself to her people and gained affection from the rest of the world. As the hereditary head of State for Great Britain and Ireland, and Head of the Commonwealth, she has symbolic and formal functional responsibilities but no direct political powers.

The Queen understands that the Commonwealth bears no resem-blance to the Empires of the past, but rather was built by friendship, loyalty, and the plenary desire for freedom and peace. What began as a small group of eight members: Britain, Canada, Australia, New Zealand, South Africa, Pakistan, Ceylon, and India, grew to fifty-four nations at the beginning of the twenty-first century.

The commonwealth embraces developed, developing, and underde-veloped countries, large and small from all regions of the world except the Middle East. The Commonwealth shares a common English lan-guage and serves as a forum for the promotion of good government, education, economic development, and human rights. The Queen and her family perform countless individual, community, and state formalities, and provide valuable support for over six-hundred public and private charities that vary widely from helping children to preserving the environment.[59]

During her reign, Queen Elizabeth was the last monarch to work directly with Prime Minister Winston Churchill and the first to receive the first Pope (John Paul II) to visit the U.K. Her government, led by Margaret Thatcher, contributed invaluable support in working with U.S. President Ronald Reagan and U.S.S.R. General Secretary Mikhail Gorbachev in circumstances that led to the fall of the Berlin Wall and the end of the Cold War. The most influential rock band in the world, The Beatles, released their first album during her reign and her government handed Hong Kong over to the Chinese after one-hundred-fifty-five years of English rule. She will go down in history as the only British monarch who was in office when the U.K. both joined the European Community and then shockingly after forty-three years of membership, voted to exit the political-economic European Union. As of September 2015, Queen Elizabeth has made two-hundred-fifty-six overseas visits to one-hundred-sixteen countries over the course of her reign.[60]

As the Queen of England, she also holds the title of Supreme Governor of the Church of England and is symbolically authoritative in the Church of Scotland. Her primary role in this regard is to appoint archbishops, bishops, and deans recommended by the prime minister. While she can't reject the prime minister's advice, she can raise questions and ask for more information. She is Anglican, a denomination of the Episcopalian faith, and holds an honorary membership in the Church of Scotland, a Presbyterian denomination. The Queen

---

[59] Sally Bedell Smith, *Elizabeth The Queen*, (Random House, New York, NY), 100.

[60] Sara Kettler, *Queen Elizabeth II*, (Bio Magazine).

has continuously expressed a deep commitment to her church and the principles of Christianity.

If you look at the coin with the Queen's portrait, you will see the inscription "Elizabeth II D.G. REG. F.D." This stands for *"Elizabeth II Dei Gratia Regina Fidei Defensor,"* translated as *"Elizabeth II, by the Grace of God, Queen, Defender of the Faith."* This is no mere title, but a command that she fully embraces as evidenced by her recent Christmas messages to the United Kingdom and Commonwealth nations including:

"To many of us, our beliefs are of fundamental importance. For me, the teachings of Christ and my own personal accountability before God provide a framework in which I try to lead my life. I, like so many of you, have drawn great comfort in difficult times from Christ's words and example (2000)."

"I know just how much I rely on my own faith to guide me through the good times and the bad. Each day is a new beginning, I know that the only way to live my life is to try to do what is right, to take the long view, to give of my best in all that the day brings, and to put my trust in God. Like others of you who draw inspiration from your own faith, I draw strength from the message of hope in the Christmas gospel (2002)."

"Although we are capable of great acts of kindness, history teaches us that we sometimes need saving from ourselves, from our recklessness or our greed. God sent in the world a unique person, neither a philosopher nor a general, important though they are, but a Savior, with the power to forgive. Forgiveness lies at the heart of the Christian faith. It can heal broken families, it can restore friendships, and it can reconcile divided communities. It is forgiveness that we feel the power of God's love...It is my prayer that on this Christmas day we might all find room in our lives for the message of the angels and for the love of God through Christ our Lord (2011)."[61]

---

[61] Rob Price, *Briefing on Life of Queen Elizabeth* (Business Insider Australia).

Queen Elizabeth II is an example of what biblical scripture calls living in this world, but not being of this world. She regards her faith as duty, not a sense of burden. Her faith is also part of the rhythm of her daily life. She has the capacity of leadership fueled by the power of the Holy Spirit, living her faith to take anything that the world throws at her. Everything in life for Queen Elizabeth II, is ordered from her theology and all-encompassing relationship with God. She worships unfailingly every Sunday and receives Communion several times during the year, mainly at Christmas, Easter, and Whitsunday, the Christian festival of Pentecost. She treasures Anglicism, loves the Book of Prayers that originated in AD 1662, and has called the King James Version Bible a masterpiece of English prose.[62]

She lacks the power to govern and at the same time has the positive power of influence. Her faith and moral behavior set a high standard for service and citizenship by rewarding achievement and carrying out her pledge of life-long service that she made on her twenty-first birthday. She does not regret and has only love for her faith, dominion, and citizens around the world. She connects to Adam and her family history represents but one family under God.

The Crown and Cross

This narrative began in ancient times and encompasses ninety-five kings and queens, up to and including Queen Elizabeth II. *The Adam Connection* symbolizes humankind connections in the story of one family. Literary non-fiction writers usually refrain from using actual symbols to represent historical events, because a symbol can potentially mislead or misrepresent events in the narrative.

Not in this case. There are symbols that can profoundly represent the events in *The Adam Connection*. The ancestry story begins with

---

[62] Sally Bedell Smith, Ibid, 264.

God, continues with Adam, and ends with Queen Elizabeth II. There are uniquely two symbols that can capture or symbolize much or most of this recorded history. Those symbols would be the "Crown" and the "Cross."

A crown is a symbolic headgear that is typically worn by monarch. This ornamental headgear represents power, glory, immortality, royalty, and sovereignty. It is often made from precious metals such as gold and decorated with jewels like diamonds. Some believe the use of crowns originated with the Persian Rulers in the sixth century B.C. In the tenth century B.C., David, second King of Israel and Judah, referred to a crown in his instructions about the godly life during the reign of God.

In European countries which are based on Christian tradition, a monarch's power is given from the power of the church. That is why, when a new monarch is crowned, a crown is placed on a monarch's head by a church official. The British are one of the few monarchies in the world that continues a tradition of coronation, although Britain is not the only monarchy that uses a crown as a national symbol.[63] "You welcomed him with rich blessings and placed a crown of pure gold on his head" (Psalm 21:3).

Queen Elizabeth II wore the seventeenth-century St. Edward's crown at her coronation, with the crown representing the power of her monarchy and connection with God. The Crown also represents the sovereign state to which the British Commonwealth owes a form of allegiance. Each British monarch believes they have the divine right of Kings to rule their people.

Adam was created on the sixth day by God, the Creator, and King of the Universe. His creation of Adam in his own image was the Crown of Creation, so much so, that on the seventh day, God had finished

---

[63] *History of Crowns, Origin and Symbolism of Crown. History of Hats.*

His work and He rested. God blessed the seventh day and made it divine. The sovereignty of God incorporates His supreme authority and power. Therefore, the crown symbolically associated with the King of the Universe is emblematically associated with Adam and all the kings and queens up to and including Queen Elizabeth II in this one family under God.

There is another symbol that represents the essence of this story and that is the Celtic Cross. While the Celtic Cross is today a symbol for Irish culture and faith, its true heritage could very well originate back to the twenty-fourth century BC in Scythia when the third generation of Noah became known as the Gaels or Celts, a Caucasian tribe that descended over the next 4,300 years to form much of the ancient and modern Asian, Middle Eastern, European, and North American races.

The Celtic Cross is believed to have meaning in both Christianity and Paganism beginning with its early symbolism of Taranis, the god of thunder, and an even earlier representation of the Roman sun god, Invictus. The Celtic Cross is said to have been introduced by St. Patrick, the fifth century Roman Catholic missionary and bishop who brought Christianity to Ireland. In this regard, the cross represents Christianity and the circle is the Celtic representation of eternity where there is no beginning or end. St. Patrick is said to have been mindful of the Irish Pagan traditions and in his conversion of the country, accommodated the Celtic Cross as a symbol that would neatly bridge the Pagan-Christian divide. Make no mistake, the Celtic Crosses that were made in Ireland, Scotland, and Wales from the fifth century onwards, were made by Christians for the glory of God.

Some say the Celtic Cross, including its intricate circular design, represents the four directions of north, south, east, and west, while others suggest the cross represents the four elements being earth, air, fire, and water. Still others believe the cross depicts stages of the day:

morning, noon, evening, and midnight. Another possibility for some spiritualists is the representation of self, wisdom, nature, and divinity. Today, an Irish Catholic priest would have no difficulty in explaining that the circle on the cross represents the eternal nature of God's love.

The Christian cross symbolizes the religion of Christianity. It represents and memorializes the death of Jesus Christ by crucifixion on a cross. The empty cross is usually favored by Protestant Christians while Catholic and Orthodox Christians favor the crucifix with Jesus on it.

It is the "Crown" and the "Cross" that symbolize *The Adam Connection*—a story 6,000 years in the making from the King of the Universe to the Queen of England. The crown of Creation to the crown of a monarch. It is an ancestral story that began with Adam who sinned against God, followed by 144 generations of sinners who worshiped many gods, no gods, and one true God. From the Celtic cross that represented ancient and medieval times to the Christian cross that originated in the second century, the cross unites Christian believers worldwide including the British monarchy.

Pragmaticaly, while a symbol can never have a definite meaning, it can be very real if that is what a person believes to be true.

Chapter 15

The Essence of Belief

The essence, spirit, and soul of belief is defined as something that one accepts as true or real. Belief is a firmly held opinion or conviction about something, even in the abstract. The concept of essence is considered an intentionally logical and commonsense point of view. Belief is an acceptance that a statement is true or that something exists.

Deliberations about faith, belief, and reason using rational arguments stretch back in history to the times of Moses, Jesus, Mohamed, and the great theologians and philosophers including Saint Augustine and Thomas Aquinas. Since the sixteenth century and advent of the scientific revolution, explorations of theology and science have converged in a novel and creative manner. In Europe, theology was then considered the "Queen of the Sciences." Augustine defined theology as anything to do with knowledge of the secular world and Aquinas considered theology a science because it considers special and general revelation of knowledge. He believed not only is knowledge based on the perception of the senses, but that same belief leads to faith and to a way to know the truth.[64],[65]

---

[64] *Augustine*, Internet Encyclopedia of Philosophy.

[65] *Aquinas: Philosophical Theology*, Internet Encyclopedia of Philosophy.

Throughout the ages, humankind has sought to understand the truth about faith and the development of personal belief. Scientists such as Galileo and Isaac Newton were men of strong religious beliefs even as they revealed world-changing discoveries that dominated mathematics, astronomy, and physics. Isaac Newton authored more writings on biblical interpretations than all his groundbreaking contributions to mathematics and physics combined.

In response to a question about the greatest commandment revealed by God to Moses and the Israelites, Jesus replied, "Love the Lord your God with all your heart and with all your soul and with all your mind" (Matthew 23:37 NIV). So, here we have a recording of Jesus Christ, in an ancient historical book (Bible), that many believe is the inerrant, infallible word of God, exhorting humankind to love God with "all your mind."

It seems to me that science was never intended to be separate from faith and belief. Humanity's search for the truth is enhanced when we open our minds to the convergence of science and belief, without intended or unintended prejudice, malice, or ill will towards others.

The British political theorist and philosopher John Locke is highly regarded as one of the most influential thinkers of the seventeenth century and a person who had significant influence on the writers of the United States Declaration of Independence. Locke believed there is no truth more evident than the existence of God, the Creator and eternal being. Locke professed that belief is based on attaining understanding by way of sensing, perceiving, and thinking.[66]

Blaise Pascal, the seventeenth century French physicist, mathematician, philosopher, and theologian, was a brilliant and passionate seeker of truth. Pascal believed that the truth could be achieved by

---

[66] *Locke*, Internet Encyclopedia of Philosophy.

incorporating reason, belief, and faith. He poignantly stated that we cannot only know the truth by reason, but also by our heart. The heart is how we know the first principles of truth. The famous "Pascal's Wager" is an argument in philosophy which advocates that all humans bet with their lives in a belief that God exists or that he does not.[67]

Ludwig Feuerbach (1989), the nineteenth century German philosopher and atheist, did in fact bet against the existence of God with his sharp criticisms of Christianity as a religion. However, he also believed that man exists to will, love, and think. He also believed the divine trinity in man, above the individual man, is the unity of love, will, and reason. Feuerbach held that Christianity, as a belief in God, was a fixed idea and had in fact long vanished not only from the reason, but from the life of humankind. His notion of reason inspired other Western philosophers to develop new ways of thinking about reason and belief.

Also in the nineteenth century, Scottish philosopher James Frederick Ferrier introduced the word epistemology, which is the study of knowledge and how it relates to truth, justification, and belief. In epistemology, belief refers to personal attitudes towards true or false ideas and concepts. A personal belief does not necessarily require self-analysis and caution. For example, we do not need to think about whether there will be a sunrise, we just assume and believe the sun will rise. Another example of personal belief and epistemology relates to the theory that knowledge is justified true belief. One must only believe the proposed truth and have good reason for doing so.[68]

Later in the twentieth century, a school of thought emerged about the idea that belief in God is a properly basic belief. This philosophy of religion is a reformed epistemology advocated by a group of Protestant Christian

---

[67] *Pascal's Wager About God*, Internet Encyclopedia of Philosophy.

[68] *James Frederick Ferrier*, Internet Encyclopedia of Philosophy.

philosophers, most notably, American Dr. Alvin Plantinga. Plantinga is a fellow of the American Academy of Arts and Sciences and widely regarded as one of the world's most important living Christian philosophers.

In his book, *God and Other Minds (1967)*, Plantinga argued if belief in another person's unproven mind is rational, then belief in God is also rational. In this regard, faith supplements rationality because the scope of rational human knowledge is limited in nature. In his lecture, *Two Dozen (Or So) Theistic Arguments*, Plantinga pragmatically argued that people can know the existence of God as a basic belief requiring no argument. He also reasoned that something is true if the person believes it is true based on their intent. He called out the absurdity of believing that the beauty, order, and complexity of the universe could have just happened by chance. Plantinga simply stated that there is sufficient reason to believe that the universe and wonders of Creation were designed by God.

What may be the truth for one person may be different than the truth for another. This concept of comparative truth can lead to a more modern and practical description that we might call "personal truth." Of course, personal truth would be pragmatic because it deals with things sensibly and realistically in a way that is practical rather than theoretical. A person's consideration of truth about anything can be practically considered their personal truth. While personal truth may be sufficient for some, for believers in God, it is all about faith.

"Now faith is confidence in what we hope for and assurance about what we do not see" (Hebrews 11:1 NIV).

Given that faith and belief in God is an intellectually honest pursuit, the pragmatist William James says the hope that is true is sufficient reason to believe.

Conclusion

Your Belief

The *Adam Connection* is an extraordinary story of generational love, battles, and blessings since the beginning of recorded history. The battles have been dark and evil. The blessings have been bright and hopeful. Despite the many contradictions, it is the love of this one family under God that has endured.

Imagine what a wonderful world it would be if we all loved everyone and everyone loved us in return. Imagine again what a wonderful world it would be if we respected everyone and everyone respected us in return. Let's imagine then for just a moment, what a wonderful world it would be if we connected with everyone and everyone connected with us in return. You know, the kind of connection that a mother has with her newborn child and best friends have for each other; a connection that can't be completely understood, but they just know they are connected. I believe that this kind of love, respect, and connection has in fact existed within and between generations since the beginning of time.

Unfortunately, this wonderful world is also filled with people who hate and are hated in return. Many do not respect and are not respected. Others are disconnected and in return experience no connection. The kind of disconnection that a child has from an absent mother or father, and enemies may feel for each other; a disconnection that causes a person to withdraw because of emotional or physical distress. I also believe that this kind of hate, disrespect, and disconnection has existed within and between generations, unfortunately because of the fall of man and original sin, since the beginning of time.

> *So, it begs some questions that can only be answered based on your personal belief.*
> *Do you choose to believe primarily in the natural world or the supernatural world of God?*
> *Are you ignorant about your connection with past generations?*
> *Do you think your ancestors just appeared mysteriously in the past or do your ancestors connect you with everyone else in the world?*
> *Do you know where you came from?*

In today's multicultural pluralistic society, many people believe in God and are **in** the natural world, not **of** the natural world. They draw their strength, courage, and convictions from God, and not from the natural world. There are others who choose to be **of** the natural world, and draw their strength, courage, and convictions from the world. If you are that person, you likely have chosen a world not of God. You may find yourself disconnected from God. You may possibly be more interested in science as your religion and knowingly or unknowingly stake your eternal life on the empirical evidence of what you know.

This group of people are either unsure or do not believe that God exists. For those people, personal beliefs may be spiritual, but not of God.

Then there are some others who consciously reject the existence of God. Evolutionist Stephen Hawking says that the universe seems to have been specifically designed for us and if we knew why the universe existed, then we would know the mind of God.

Even though the mind of God is unknowable, most people are seeking to know God or know Him more intimately. For those people, God's existence is not in question. Those people seek to understand God and grow closer to Him. For example, Christians choose a personal relationship with Jesus Christ and believe that through Him they will receive eternal salvation.

The Creation of God is beyond human understanding. It is impossible to ponder ten trillion galaxies in the known universe and fully understand Creation. While most scientists agree that the earth was formed about 4.5 billion years ago, creationists believe the earth is just 10,000 years old. Scientists believe human evolution began from a single cell organism within the past 3.8 billion years and that the human species evolved from Africa during the past 200,000 years. On the other hand, many religious people believe humanity began within the past 10,000 years from the creation of a man named Adam. Many of these people either are convicted in their belief or uncertain if Adam was in fact the first human being.

Then there is a third perspective that is *The Adam Connection.* This third perspective describes an evidence-based, enduring love story of battles and blessings over 144 generations during a period of more than 6,000 years. This story began with the first person created by God, His name was Adam and his date of birth was October 23, 4004 BC. Regrettably, there are many contradictions between science, religion, reason, and understanding about God.

While Mr. Darwin's origin theory has been overwhelmingly accepted by the scientific community, the theory is considered mathematically impossible. Even some of his enthusiastic apologists acknowledge that evolution is unproved and unprovable. Many others believe that evolution is neither fact, theory nor hypothesis. It is nothing more than a belief. Society is not biology. Again, there are many contractions between science, religion, reason, and understanding about the origins of man.

Depending on your worldview, recorded history is considered to cover a span of either five or six thousand years. Prevailing wisdom says that the earliest dates of recorded history can only be approximate and depend on the interpretative theories of scientists and religious scholars. Some believe that the *Holy Bible, Annals of The World,* and the *Irish Chronicles* are source documents based on mythical legends. On the other hand, these same documents have been extensively scrutinized and considered by many scholars to be historically accurate. While science can collaborate much of recorded history, it cannot prove the authenticity or accuracy of these recordings. Again, there are many contradictions between science, religion, reason, and understanding about the records of history.

The truth is that most people in the world believe that God exists. Pragmatism tells us that belief in God is not only reasonable, it is justifiable. Pragmatists consider thought as a tool for prediction, problem solving, and action. Pragmatism argues that philosophies such as knowledge, concepts, meaning, beliefs, and science are best considered in terms of their practical use and success. Pragmatism can be a way to overcome the irreconcilable clash of temperaments between two ways of thinking, such as the claims of scientists on one hand and the morality of religion on the other.

The temperament of tough-minded people, such as scientists, have an empirical commitment to experience and the facts. The temperament of tender-minded people is inclined more towards principles and tend to be idealistic, optimistic, and religious. Tough-minded people are more skeptical and unbelieving. Tender-minded people are more dogmatic and believing. There are many contradictions between science, religion, reason, and understanding about the philosophy of pragmatism.

The essence of belief is defined as something that one accepts to be true or real. Belief is a deeply held opinion or conviction about something, even in the abstract, like believing in God. Deliberations about faith, belief, and reason stretch far back in monotheist religious history to Moses (Judaism), Jesus (Christianity), and Islam (Mohammed), and to theologians and philosophers such as Saint Augustine and Thomas Aquinas. In sixteenth century Europe, theology was considered the "Queen of Sciences."

Throughout the ages, humankind has tried to understand the truth about faith and development of personal belief. Some say that science is a belief. Only 5.5 percent of biological scientists surveyed at the National Academy of Sciences believe that God exists compared to over 83 percent of the public. World-renowned physician and geneticist Dr. Francis Collins, pragmatically states that there will never be scientific proof of God's existence. Aquinas believed that knowledge is based on perception, and that belief leads to faith and a way to know the truth. Still, there are many contradictions between science, religion, reason, and understanding about belief.

Scientists believe they know much about everything in the known universe and at the same time, they know nothing about who created the universe. Science has provided much insight about the natural world and has awkwardly and contentiously provided very little understanding about the supernatural. By comparison, religion has provided much insight about the supernatural world and at times clumsily struggles to define where it fits in the natural world, especially since the Age of Enlightenment. I believe God is "truth" and the truth is His alone. Man-made "truth" is only true to the extent such truth is inspired and revealed by God. I do not believe there is any reasonable justification for science to be the final authority about God's existence.

So, after 144 generations since Adam, covering history over a period of more than 6,000 years, you have a choice to make. What do you believe? Is *The Adam Connection* believable or at the very least plausible? Does this pragmatic narrative which connects Adam to Queen Elizabeth II, explain your own story and how you and your family may also connect to Adam? More importantly, if you can connect with Adam, can you also imagine how everyone connects to him and how you therefore connect to everyone else in the world? In this interconnected story, our friends, acquaintances, and strangers are not just other people, they are "One Family Under God."

Truthfully, I believe this one unanticipated account can in fact connect today's and subsequent generations to Adam. I believe that this one epic narrative reasonably and justifiably connects every person who has ever lived—more than an estimated one-hundred billion people since the beginning of recorded history.[69] Realistically, I believe it is impossible to have a relationship or connect with persons of the ancient past, especially if their existence is based on contradicting radiometric dating technologies, paleontology, anthropology, and archaeology. How can a person relate to an artifact other than by curiosity or intellectual interest? Such a connection may move the mind or emotions, but it cannot move the heart. It is not a relationship. These widely accepted scientific beliefs are not personally relatable nor do they provide meaning or purpose. While science is a magnificent God-given gift to humankind, it is just science. It is science that studies the natural world based on facts from observations and experiments. Science is unqualified to study the supernatural existence of God, because such study is unprovable.

For those who believe in God and are open to a very real connection to the first man created in His image, I believe you are enhancing

---

[69] Population Reference Bureau. *How Many People Have Ever Lived?*

your journey to live a life with meaning and purpose. If you believe in this divine connection, then be prepared to transform your mind, heart, and spirit. *The Adam Connection* may either strengthen your relationship with God, or you may now have a compelling reason to seek such a relationship.

The religion of Islam invites you to have a relationship with Allah, learn more about the prophet Mohammed, and join a local mosque if that is what you believe. Judaism invites you to have a relationship with God, learn more about their faith, and join a synagogue if that is what you believe. Christians encourage you to invite the Holy Spirit into your heart and accept Jesus Christ as your personal Lord and Savior. The religion of Christianity invites you to join a Catholic parish or a Bible-based Protestant church, so that you can be unconditionally loved and inspired to love God with all your heart, mind, and soul, and love the people of humanity as God loves you.

Our world community grows smaller every day and understanding is the only place where peace, joy, and happiness can find a home. Advances in science and religion must be matched by comparable advances in human relationships. I believe it is only with a strong vertical relationship with God that we can have equally strong horizontal relationships with others. Understanding brings respect and respect leads to love and the only power that can truly connect each of us with each other. It starts with belief.

I will bring *The Adam Connection* drama to a close by reflecting on God's wisdom, power, and love. I'm reminded that Moses wrote that God keeps His covenant and His loving kindness will continue for thousands of generations with those who love Him and keep His commandments (Deuteronomy 7:9).

Have you not known? Have you not heard? The everlasting God, the Lord, the Creator of the ends of the earth, neither faints nor is weary. His understanding is unsearchable. He gives power to the weak, and to those who have no might he increases strength. Even the youths shall faint and be weary, and the young men shall utterly fall, but those who wait on the Lord shall renew their strength; they shall mount up with wings like eagles, they shall run and not be weary, they shall walk and not be faint. (Isaiah 40:28-31 NKJV)

In conclusion, we consider the words of King David of Israel, the tenth century BC warrior, lyricist, and musician who wrote many of the psalms in the Book of Psalms in the Bible. He was just as honorable in battle as he was in civil and criminal justice. He spoke about the goodness, truth, power, and wisdom of God by writing, "For the word of the Lord is right, and all his work is done in truth. He loves righteousness and justice; The earth is full of the goodness of the Lord. By the word of the Lord the heavens were made, and all the host of them by the breath of his mouth. He gathers the waters of the sea together as a heap; He lays up the deep in storehouses. Let all the earth fear the Lord; let all the inhabitants of the world respect Him. For He spoke and it was done; He commanded, and it stood fast" (Psalm 33:4-9 NKJV).

One last question: What do you believe and where did you come from?

About the Author

Rob Faw is a board-certified master Christian life coach, author, and entrepreneur with global executive management experience at private and public companies doing business in North America, Latin America, Europe, and Asia Pacific. He was previously on the board of a palliative care social benefit company and board member of a non-profit family counseling organization. Rob was formerly Chapter President of an international Christian Business Leadership organization. He currently works with non-profit organizations in support of their faith-based missions in the U.S. and international. Rob has a graduate degree in global leadership from the University of San Diego and a business degree from the University of South Florida.

His previous book *World's Best Value, Global Competition in the Information Age* is about organizational excellence, leadership, and the unlimited capacity of the human spirit. Rob is a research fellow with The Arthur C. Custance Centre for Science and Christianity. He has written about Christian Ethics in the workplace and his academic paper, *Business in the 21st Century* is about intelligent leadership. He is a certified master Christian life coach with the Board of Christian Life Coaching and a member of the International Christian Coaching Association. Rob is an Ironman athlete and has competed in over forty marathons. He is a U.S. Air Force veteran. He has lived and worked in Toronto, London, Chicago, and the Silicon Valley. Rob resides with his wife Jill in Safety Harbor, Florida.

Contact: rob@robfaw.com

Appendix

Table:

Generational Men and Women in One Family Under God

1) Adam	37) Heremon	73) Finnlogha	109) Malcolm I
2) Seth	38) Irial	74) Fionn	110) Kenneth II
3) Enosh	39) Eithrial	75) Eochaidh	111) Malcom II
4) Cainan	40) Follach	76) Breas	112) Beatrix
5) Mahalaleel	41) Tighernmhas	77) Lugaidh	113) Duncan I
6) Jared	42) Enbotha	78) Crimthann	114) Malcolm III
7) Enoch	43) Simorgoill	79) Feredach	115) David I
8) Methuselah	44) Fiacha	80) Fiachadh	116) Henry
9) Lamech	45) Aengus	81) Tuathal	117) David
10) Noah	46) Maen	82) Feidimidh	118) Isobel
11) Japheth	47) Rothechtaid	83) Conn	119) Robert
12) Magog	48) Deman	84) Art	120) Robert
13) Boath	49) Dian Dain	85) Cormac	121) Robert
14) Fenius	50) Sirna	86) Cairbre	122) Marjorie
15) Niul	51) Olioll	87) Fiacha	123) Robert II
16) Gaodhal	52) Giallchaidh	88) Tireach	124) Robert III
17) Asruth	53) Nuadhat	89) Eochaidh	125) James I
18) Sruth	54) Aedhan	90) Niall	126) James II
19) Heber	55) Simeon	91) Eoghan	127) James III
20) Baouman	56) Muireadhach	92) Eochaidh	128) James IV

21) Ogaman	57) Fiach	93) Ercc	129) James V
22) Tait	58) Duach	94) Fergus	130) Mary
23) Agnon	59) Eochaidh	95) Domangart	131) James VI
24) Lamhfionn	60) Ugaine	96) Gabhra	132) Elizabeth
25) Heber	61) Cobhthach	97) Edhan	133) Sophia
26) Agnan	62) Melghe	98) Eochaidh	134) George I
27) Febric	63) Irereo	99) Domnall	135) George II
28) Nenuall	64) Connla	100) Domangart	136) Frederick
29) Nuadhad	65) Oilioll	101) Eochaid	137) George III
30) Alladh	66) Eochaidh	102) Eochaid	138) Edward
31) Arcadh	67) Aenghus	103) Adon	139) Victoria
32) Deag	68) Enna	104) Eochaid	140) Edward VII
33) Brath	69) Labraidh	105) Alpin	141) George V
34) Breoghan	70) Blathacht	106) Kenneth	142) Edward VIII
35) Bile	71) Essamain	107) Constantine I	143) George VI
36) Galamh	72) Roignein	108) Donald II	144) Elizabeth II

Bibliography

Aardsma, G.A. (1989). Myths Regarding Radiocarbon Dating. Dallas, TX. Acts & Facts.

Ancient History Before Christ or Before the Common Era. (2015). Published online by Sandbox Networks, Inc. as Fact Monster.

Augustine. Internet Encyclopedia of Philosophy. Retrieved from http://www.iep.utm.edu/augustin/

Aquinas: Philosophical Theology. Internet Encyclopedia of Philosophy. Retrieved from http://www.iep.utm.edu/aq-ph-th/

Aquinas, Saint Thomas. (1924). The Summa Contra Gentiles of St. Thomas Aquinas. London, England. Burns Oates & Washbourne Ltd.

Aquinas, Saint Thomas. (1921). The Summa Theologica. London, England. Burns Oates & Washbourne Ltd.

Barrett, David A. (1982). World Christian Encyclopedia. Oxford, England. Oxford University Press.

Bartholomew, Craig G. and Goheen, Michael W. (2014). The Drama of Scripture, Finding Our Place in the Biblical Story, Second Edition. Grand Rapids, MI. Baker

Academic.

Bennett, William J. (1995). The Moral Compass, A Companion to the Book of Virtues. New York, NY. Simon & Schuster.

Bergman, Jerry, PhD. (2015). James Ussher and His Chronology: Reasonable or Ridiculous? Acts & Facts.

Biblical Data Are Historically Testable. (2016). Published online by Institute for Creation Research.

Blackaby, Henry T. & King, Claude V. (1994). Experiencing God. Nashville, TN. Broadman & Holman Publishers.

Bloom, Jon. (2015). God's Glory in Your Extraordinary Story. Published online by Desiring God.

Book of Order. (2013). The Constitution of the Presbyterian Church (U.S.A.). Louisville, KY. The Office of the General Assembly.

Bragg, Melvyn. (2011). The Book of Books, The Radical Impact of the King James Bible 1611 – 2011. Berkley, CA. Counterpoint Press.

Brom, Robert H. (2004). The One True God. Catholic Answers. Retrieved from https://www.catholic.com/tract/the-great-heresies

Broocks, Rice. (2013). The Bible – fact or fiction? Fox News. Retrieved http://www.foxnews.com/opinion/2013/04/21/bible-fact-or-fiction.html

Brown, Ryk. (2011). Fergus Mor Macerca King of Scots. Retrieved http://wc.rootsweb.ancestry.com/cgibin/igm.cgi?op=GET&db=ryk_brown&id=I1820

Cantirino, Matthew. (2012). The Queen's Quiet Faith. First

Things. Retrieved from https://www.firstthings.com/
blogs/firstthoughts/2012/06/the-queens-quiet-faith

Carey, John. (1994). The Irish National Origin-Legend:
Synthetic Pseudohistory. Department of Anglo-Saxon,
Norse, and Celtic, University of Cambridge.

Center for Applied Research in the Apostolate. (2016). Church
Statistics.

Chiang, Dr. Gary R., PhD. (2011). Rescuing Science from
Preconceived Beliefs. Hamilton, Canada. Doorway
Publications.

Chignell, Andrew. (2010). The Ethics of Belief. Stanford
Encyclopedia of Philosophy. Retrieved from https://
plato.stanford.edu/entries/ethics-belief/

Christianity in Britain. (2011). Retrieved from http://www.
bbc.co.uk/religion/religions/christianity/history/uk_1.
shtml

Church of Scotland. (2011). BBC. Retrieved from http://
www.bbc.co.uk/religion/religions/christianity/
subdivisions/churchofscotland_1.shtml

Collins, Francis. (2004). An Interview – The Question of God.
PBS. WGBH Educational Foundation. Retrieved from
http://www.pbs.org/wgbh/questionofgod/voices/
collins.html

Copan, P. (2001). Warranted Christian Belief. Published in The
Review of Metaphysics 54.

Chaffey, Tim. (2017). 3 Evidences That Confirm the Bible
is Not Made Up. Answers in Genesis. Retrieved from
https://answersingenesis.org/is-the-bible-true/3-

evidences-confirm-bible-not-made-up/

Chilton, Bruce. (2004). Rabbi Paul, An Intellectual Biography. New York, NY. Doubleday, a division of Random House, Inc.

Chilton, Bruce. (2000). Rabbi Jesus, An Intimate Biography. New York, NY. Doubleday, a division of Random House, Inc.

Clayton, Peter, A. (2006). Chronicles of the Pharaoh's. London, England. Thames and Hudson.

Collins, Francis S. (2010). Belief, Readings on the Reason for Faith. New York, NY. Harper One.

Coolman, Robert. (2014). Keeping Time: The Origin of B.C. and A.D. Live Science. Retrieved from http://www.livescience.com/45510-anno-domini.html

Comfort, Ray. (2001). Scientific Facts in the Bible. Alachyua, FL. Bridge-Logos Publishers.

Countryman, Jack. (2009). God's Wisdom for Your Every Need. Nashville, TN. Thomas Nelson Publishing.

Craig, William Lane. (2013). Does God Exist? Reasonable Faith. Retrieved from http://www.reasonablefaith.org/does-god-exist-1

Craig, William Lane. (2015). Concept of God in Islam and Christianity. Reasonable Faith. Retrieved from http://www.reasonablefaith.org/the-concept-of-god-in-islam-and-christianity

Custance, Arthur C. (2013). Noah's Three Sons, 2nd Edition, Human History in Three Dimensions. Ancaster, Canada. Doorway Publications.

Custance, Arthur C. (2013). Is Man an Animal, 2nd Edition, The Biological Differences Between Man and Beast. Ancaster, Canada. Doorway Publications.

Donoghue, Clayton N. (2015). The Irish Empire, the Story of Niall of the Nine Hostages. Victoria, Canada. Fiesen Press.

Catholic Answers. (2011). Didn't the Catholic Church add to the Bible? Retrieved from https://www.catholic.com/qa/didnt-the-catholic-church-add-to-the-bible

Christian Class Ethereal Library. Lobegott Friedrich Konstantin Von Tischendorf (1815-1874). Biography. Retrieved from http://www.ccel.org/ccel/tischendorf

Dating Creation. Scribd. Retrieved from https://www.scribd.com/document/48257203/DATING-CREATION

Demme, Greg and Sarfati, Jonathan. (2001). Big bang critic dies (Fred Doyle). Creation Ministries International. Retrieved from http://creation.com/big-bang-critic-dies-fred-hoyle

Diversity of Beliefs about the Age of the Earth, by old-earth creationists, young-age creationists, and scientists. (2015). Religious Tolerance. Retrieved from http://www.religioustolerance.org/ev_date.htm

Dalberg-Acton, John Emerich Edward. (1988). Essays in Religion, Politics and Morality, Selected Writings of Lord Acton, edited by J. Rufus Fears. Indianapolis, IN. Liberty Fund, Inc.

Draayer, Gerald. (2009). God and War: What the Bible Says About the Just War Principle. God and Science.

Retrieved from http://www.godandscience.org/
apologetics/just_war_principle.html

Duffield, Daniel. (2013). Niall and the Irish Pirates. Liberty,
Utah. Daniel J. Duffield.

Dundee, Charles Roger. (1847). A Collation of the Sacred
Scriptures.

Dunham-Massey, John. (1918). Jeremiah, Ireland, the Stone of
Scone, and the English Kings. London, England.

Easley, Kendell H. (2002). Understanding the Bible. Nashville,
TN. Holman Bible Publishers.

Encyclopedia of Philosophy, Volume III. (1967). Macmillan,
Inc.

Encyclopedia Britannica Online. (2007).

Enosh. Bible Hub. Retrieved from http://biblehub.com/
topical/e/enos.htm

Evans, Nicholas. (2010). The Present and the Past in Medieval
Irish Chronicles. Woodbridge, UK. Boydell & Brewer
Ltd.

Faw, Robert D. (2014). Faw Family History, 3rd Edition.

Ferrier, James Frederick. Internet Encyclopedia of Philosophy.
Retrieved from http://www.iep.utm.edu/ferrier/

Feuerbach, Ludwig. (1989) The Essence of Christianity. New
York, NY. Prometheus Books.

Frankl, Viktor E. (1984). Man's Search For Meaning, An
Introduction to Logotherapy. New York, NY. Simon
and Schuster, Inc.

Funk, Cary and Rainie, Lee. (2015). Evolution and
Perceptions of Scientific Consensus. Pew Research

Center. Retrieved from http://www.pewinternet.
org/2015/01/29/public-and-scientists-views-on-
science-and-society/

Gardner, Laurence. (2002). Genesis of the Grail Kings, the
Explosive Story of Genetic Cloning and Ancient
Bloodlines of Jesus. Beverly, MA. Fair Winds Press.

Geoghegan, Eddie. (2015). The Monarchs of Ireland.
Retrieved from http://www.heraldry.ws/info/article12.
html

Geoghegan, Eddie. (2015). The Royalty of Scotland. Retrieved
from http://www.heraldry.ws/info/article11.html

George, Timothy. (2008). What do Protestant churches mean
when they recite "I believe in the holy catholic church"
and "the community of saints" in the Apostles' Creed?
Christianity Today. Retrieved from http://www.
christianitytoday.com/history/2008/september/what-
do-protestant-churches-mean-when-they-recite-i.html

Gill, Dr. A.L. (2006). God's Promises For Your Every Need.
Nashville, TN. J. Countryman, a Division of Thomas
Nelson, Inc.

Hale, Dr. William. (1830). New Analysis of Chronology and
Geography, History and Prophecy, Volume 1.

Hakedosha, Miriam. (2010). Alternative GenHist, Eochocan
and the Scottish Royal House of Athol.

Hakedosha, Miriam. (2010). Alternative Genhist, Fergs Mor
mac Earca and the Pictish Princess Royal.

Harper, Douglas. (2015). Belief. Etymology Dictionary.
Retrieved from http://www.etymonline.com/index.

php?term=belief

Harper, Richard A. Descendants of Amenhotep IV Akhenaten Pharaoh of Egypt. Alfred Larson Peterson Family Genealogy.

Harper, Richard A. Genealogy Report: Descendants of Tamar Tephi, Princess of Judah. Retrieved from http://www.genealogy.com/ftm/h/a/r/Richard-Allen-Harper/GENE3-0001.html

Harari, Yuval Noah. (2015). Sapiens, A Brief History of Humankind. New York, NY. HarperCollins Publishers.

Haub, Carl. (2011). How Many People Have Ever Lived on Earth? Population Bureau. Hawking, Stephen (1988). A Brief History of Time. London, England. Bantam Press, a division of Transworld Publishers Ltd.

History of the Monarchy. (2017). Retrieved from https://www.royal.uk/search?tags[0]=history%20of%20the%20monarchy

History of Judaism. (2009). BBC. Retrieved from www.bbc.co.uk/religion/religions/judaism/history/history_1.shtml

Holmes, Alonzo. (2012). Noah's Family, The Story of Mankind. Bloomington, IN. Xlibris, LLC.

Hookway, Christopher. (2013). Pragmatism. Stanford Encyclopedia of Philosophy. Retrieved from https://plato.stanford.edu/entries/pragmatism/

Horn, Trent. (2013). Does It Matter Than Many Scientists Are Atheists? Catholic Answers. Retrieved from https://www.catholic.com/magazine/online-edition/does-it-matter-that-many-scientists-are-atheists

Howell, Elizabeth. (2014). How Many Stars Are in the Universe? Space.com Retrieved from http://www.space.com/26078-how-many-stars-are-there.html

Hughes, David. (2007). The British Chronicles, Book Two. Westminster, MD. Heritage Books.

Huntington, Samuel P. (1996). The Clash of Civilizations and the Remaking of World Order. New York, NY. Simon & Schuster.

James, William (1975). Pragmatism and the Meaning of Truth. Cambridge, MA and London, England. Harvard University Press.

Jones, Floyd Nolen (2005). Chronology of the Old Testament. Green Forest, AR. New Leaf Publishing Group.

Jones, Roger. (2008). Philosophy and the Proof of God's Existence. Philosopher. Retrieved from http://www.philosopher.org.uk/god.htm

Jordan, Jeff. (2014). Pragmatic Arguments and Belief in God. Stanford Encyclopedia of Philosophy. Retrieved from https://plato.stanford.edu/entries/pragmatic-belief-god/notes.html

Judd, Dennis. (2012). George VI. London, England. I.B. Tauris & Co Ltd.

Johnson, Todd M. and Grim, Brian J. (2013). The World's Religions in Figures, An Introduction to International Religious Demography. Chichester, UK. John Wiley and Son's, Ltd.

Hart, D.G. (2016). The Printing Press Prophet. Wall Street

Journal. Retrieved from https://www.wsj.com/articles/
the-printing-press-prophet-1452290894

Hedges, Chris (2003). What Every Person Should Know
About War. New York Times. Retrieved from http://
www.nytimes.com/2003/07/06/books/chapters/
what-every-person-should-know-about-war.html

Heschel, Abraham Joshua. Jewish Virtual Library. Retrieved
from https://www.jewishvirtuallibrary.org/abraham-
joshua-heschel

Hirst, John. (2009). The Shortest History of Europe. Brecon,
England. Old Street Publishing, Ltd.

History of Crowns – Origin and Symbolism of Crowns.
History of Hats. Retrieved from http://www.
historyofhats.net/headgear-history/history-of-crowns/

Jeffrey, Grant R. (2010). The Signature of God. Colorado
Springs, CO. WaterBrook Press.

Keating, Geoffrey. (1983). The History of Ireland, Volume II.
Dublin, Ireland. Irish Geological Foundation.

Kennedy, Matthew. (1705). A Chronological Genealogical
and Historical Dissertation of the Royal Family of the
Stuarts. London, England. Lewis Coignard Printer and
Bookseller.

Kershaw, Tom. (2012). The Religion and Political Views of
Queen Elizabeth II. Holloverse. Retrieved from http://
hollowverse.com/elizabeth-ii/

Kettler, Sara. (2015). Queen Elizabeth II: 7 Facts on the
Longest Reigning Monarch in British History.
Biography. Retrieved from https://www.biography.

com/news/queen-elizabeth-longest-reign-celebration-monarch-facts#!

Kinley, Jeff. (2014). As It Was in The Days of Noah. Eugene, OR. Harvest House Publishers.

Kitchen, K.A. (2003). On the Reliability of the Old Testament. Grand Rapids, MI. William B. Eerdmans Publishing.

Koons, Stephanie. (2014). How many scholarly papers are on the Web? At least 114 million, professor finds. Penn State University. Retrieved from http://news.psu.edu/story/329490/2014/10/09/research/how-many-scholarly-papers-are-web-least-114-million-professor-finds

Kors, Charles Alan. (2015). Birth of the Modern Mind: The Intellectual History of the 17th and 18th Centuries. The Great Course. Retrieved from http://www.thegreatcourses.com/courses/birth-of-the-modern-mind-the-intellectual-history-of-the-17th-and-18th-centuries.html

Koukl, Greg. (2013). Is It Rational to Believe in God? Stand to Reason. Retrieved from http://www.str.org/articles/is-it-rational-to-believe-in-god#.WTMAluvyupo

Kushner, Aviya. (2015). The Lost Meaning of Biblical Names. Wall Street Journal. Retrieved from https://www.wsj.com/articles/the-lost-meanings-of-biblical-names-1449245837

Lamb, Robert. (2010). Are Scientists Atheists? Seeker. Retrieved from https://www.seeker.com/are-scientists-atheists-1765139498.html

Lamech. Bible Hub. Retrieved from http://biblehub.com/topical/l/lamech.htm

Larson, Edward J. and Witham, Larry. (1998). Leading Scientists Still Reject God. Nature, Vol. 394, No 6691, p. 313. Macmillan Publishers Ltd.

Lerer, Seth. (2015). History of the English Language. The Great Courses. Retrieved from http://www.thegreatcourses.com/courses/history-of-the-english-language-2nd-edition.html

Lewis, C.S. (1952). Mere Christianity. New York, NY. Harper Collins.

Linder, Doug. (2004). Bishop James Ussher Sets the Date for Creation. Published online by University of Missouri – Kansas City.

Lipka, Michael. (2015). Americas' faith in God may be eroding. Published online by Pew Research Center.

Lipson, H.S. (1980). "A Physicist Looks at Evolution," Physics Bulletin, vol. 31.

Listverse Staff. (2010). Top 10 Interesting Facts about the Scythians. Listverse. Retrieved from http://listverse.com/2010/01/05/top-10-interesting-facts-about-the-scythians/

Loconte, Joseph. (2015). When Luther Shook Up Christianity. Wall Street Journal. Retrieved from https://www.wsj.com/articles/when-luther-shook-up-christianity-1446159795

Locke. Internet Encyclopedia of Philosophy. Retrieved from http://www.iep.utm.edu/locke/

Lynch, Michael. (1990). A New History of Scotland. London, England. Century Limited.

Mackie, J.D. (1964). A History of Scotland. London, England. Penguin Books.

Mann, Adam. (2011). How to Picture the Size of the Universe. Wired Magazine.

Mariana, Markus. (2002). Summary of Archaeological Periods. The Israeli Mosaic. Retrieved from http://mosaic. lk.net/timeline.html

Mariana, Markus. (2002). Timeline of Israeli History in Short. The Israeli Mosaic. Retrieved from http://mosaic. lk.net/timeline.html

Mark, Joshua J. (2015). Ireland. Ancient History Encyclopedia. Retrieved from http://www.ancient.eu/ireland/

Mark, Joshua J. (2014). Daily Life in Ancient Mesopotamia. Ancient History Encyclopedia. Retrieved from http:// www.ancient.eu/article/680/

Marshall, Rosalind K. (2008). John Knox. Edinburgh, Scotland. Birlinn Limited.

Masci, David. (2009). Scientists and Belief. Pew Research Center. Retrieved from http://www.pewforum. org/2009/11/05/an-overview-of-religion-and-science-in-the-united-states/

Massie, Allan. (2010). The Royal Stuarts, A History of the Family That Shaped Britain. New York, NY. St. Martin's Press.

Maxwell, Arthur. (1994). The Bible Story. Hagerstown, MD. Review and Herald Publishing Association.

McLaughlin, Ra. (2015). Which is the True Church? Third Millennium Ministries. Retrieved from http://reformedanswers.org/answer.asp/file/40239

Metaxas, Eric. (2015). Miracles. New York, NY. Penguin Random House LLC.

McCourt, Malachy. (2004). History of Ireland. Philadelphia, PA. Running Press Book Publishers.

McDonald, Suzanne. (2013). John Knox for Armchair Theologians. Louisville, KY. Westminster John Knox Press.

McGough, Hugh. (2012). Irish Kings. The University College Cork. Celt Corpus of Electronic Texts.

McGough, Hugh. (2014). Scots Kings, Including Kings of Dál Riata Who Reigned from Ireland. Magoo. Retrieved from http://magoo.com/hugh/scotskings.html

Milesisus of Spain, King of Braganza, Father of Irish Race, The High Kings of Ireland. Ancestry. Retrieved from http://freepages.genealogy.rootsweb.ancestry.com/~cnoelldunc/Ancient/Milesius/A1.htm

Millman, J., Taylor B. and Effron L. (2012). Evidence Noah's Biblical Flood Happened, Says Robert Ballard. ABC News. Retrieved from http://abcnews.go.com/Technology/evidence-suggests-biblical-great-flood-noahs-time-happened/story?id=17884533

Meyer, G.J. (2006). A World Undone, The Story of the Great War, 1914–1918. New York, NY. Bantam Dell, a division of Random House, Inc.

Moody, Steve. God is Love. Life, Hope, and Truth. Retrieved

from https://lifehopeandtruth.com/god/who-is-god/
god-is-love/

Moore, Charles. (2015). The Secret of Queen Elizabeth II's
Record Reign: Faith, Patience and a Touch of Cunning.
The Telegraph. Retrieved from http://www.telegraph.
co.uk/news/uknews/queen-elizabeth-II/11845161/
The-secret-of-Queen-Elizabeth-IIs-record-reign-
outstripping-Victoria.html

Morris, Henry Ph.D. and Clark, Martin E. (1987). The Bible
Has the Answer. Green Forest, AR. Masters Books.

Morris, Rod (2015). Fergus Mor MacErca. Retrieved from
http://www.themorrisclan.com/GENEALOGY/
FAMCHART%20A9.html

Mother of Humanity. (2015). Africa: Cradle of Civilization.
Retrieved from http://motherofhumanity.org/mother-
of-humanity-africa-project/africa-cradle-of-civilization/

Moyers, Bill (1996). Genesis, A Living Conversation. New
York, NY 10036. Doubleday.

O'Brien, J, Irish-English Dictionary 2nd ed., Dublin:
Hodges and Smith, 1832. Retrieved from http://
askaboutireland.ie/learning-zone/secondary-students/
irish/labhairt-agus-scriobh/ebooks-as-gaeilge/obrien-
irish-english-dict/

O'Donovan, John. (1856). Annals of the Four Masters.
Dublin, Ireland. Hodges, Smith and Co.

O'Neil, Dennis. (2012). Pre-Darwinian Theories. Palomar
College. Retrieved from http://anthro.palomar.edu/
evolve/evolve_1.htm

O'Hart, John. (1892). Irish Pedigrees or the Origins and Stem of the Irish Nation, 5th Edition, Volume 1. Dublin, Ireland. Jane Duffy and Co. Ltd.

Parnell, Jonathan. (2015). God's Grace Will Find You. Desiring God. Retrieved from http://www.desiringgod.org/articles/god-s-grace-will-find-you

Pascals Wager About God. Internet Encyclopedia of Philosophy. Retrieved from http://www.iep.utm.edu/pasc-wag/

Paul, John II. (1994). Crossing the Threshold of Hope. New York, NY. Alfred A. Knopf, Inc.

Paul, John II. (2003). Go in Peace, A Gift of Enduring Love. Chicago, IL. Loyola Press.

Pearson, J.J. (1924). Tamar Tephi: or the Maid of Destiny. London, England.

Phillips, Francis. (2012). More Than Any Monarch, Queen Elizabeth II Understands the Spiritual Element of her Coronation Oath. Catholic Herald. Retrieved from http://www.catholicherald.co.uk/commentandblogs/2012/02/07/more-than-any-monarch-queen-elizabeth-ii-understands-the-spiritual-element-of-her-coronation-oath/

Pierce, Larry and Marion. (2003). The Annals of the World, James Ussher's Classic Survey of World History. Green Forest, AR. Masters Books, Inc.

Piper, John. (1980). God Created Us for His Glory. Desiring God. Retrieved from http://www.desiringgod.org/messages/god-created-us-for-his-glory

Piper, John. (2012). I Am Who I Am. Desiring God. Retrieved from http://www.desiringgod.org/messages/i-am-who-i-am--2

Piper, John. (2015). Ten Reasons to Revel in Being Chosen. Desiring God. Retrieved from http://www.desiringgod.org/articles/ten-reasons-to-revel-in-being-chosen

Piper, John. (1976). The Glory of God as the Goal of History. Desiring God. Retrieved from http://www.desiringgod.org/articles/the-glory-of-god-as-the-goal-of-history

Piper, John. (2015). This is the Best of Times, And the Worst of Times. Desiring God. Retrieved from http://www.desiringgod.org/articles/this-is-the-best-of-times-and-the-worst-of-times

Plantinga, Alvin. (1981). Is Belief in God Properly Basic? Calvin College. Published in Nous, Vol. 15, No.1.

Plantinga, Alvin. (2015). Two-Dozen (Or So) Theistic Arguments. Lecture Calvin College. Retrieved from http://www.calvin.edu/academic/philosophy/virtual_library/articles/plantinga_alvin/two_dozen_or_so_theistic_arguments.pdf

Population Bureau. How Many People Have Every Lived? Retrieved from http://www.prb.org/Publications/Articles/2002/HowManyPeopleHaveEverLivedonEarth.aspx

Porter, Noah, editors. (1913). Epistemology. Webster's Revised Unabridged Dictionary. G&C Merriam Company.

Price, Rob. (2015). The Death of Queen Elizabeth Will Be the Most Disruptive Event in Britain in the Last 70 Years.

Published online by Business Insider Australia.

Princess Tea Tamara Tephi. (2015). Star of David. Retrieved from http://www.star-of-david.net/princess-tea-tamara-tephi.html

Principles of Scientific Creationism. (2015). Institute for Creation Research. Retrieved from http://www.icr.org/article/Creationism-Principles/

Public Broadcasting System. (2004). NOVA – How Did Life Begin? Retrieved from http://www.pbs.org/wgbh/nova/evolution/how-did-life-begin.html

Public Broadcasting System. (2004). Question of God. Retrieved from http://www.pbs.org/wgbh/questionofgod/voices/collins.html

Quammen, David. (2004). Was Darwin Wrong? National Geographic. Retrieved from http://ngm.nationalgeographic.com/ngm/0411/feature1/fulltext.html

Reaoch, Stacy. (2015). Five Ways Children Will Change the World. Desiring God. Retrieved from http://www.desiringgod.org/articles/five-ways-children-will-change-the-world

Reed, Robert. (1995). The First Blast of the Trumpet Against the Monstrous Regiment of Women. Dallas, Texas. Presbyterian Heritage Publications.

Reinke, Tony. (2015). Why Do I Exist? Desiring God. Retrieved from http://www.desiringgod.org/articles/why-do-i-exist

Religious Tolerance. Estimate of the Age of Earth. Retrieved from http://www.religioustolerance.org/ev_date1.htm

Rinehart, John. (2015). What God Thinks About You. Desiring God. Retrieved from http://www.desiringgod. org/articles/what-god-thinks-about-you

Roberts, Tyler. (2015). Skeptics and Believers: Religious Debate in the Western Intellectual Tradition. The Great Courses. Retrieved from http://www. thegreatcourses.com/courses/skeptics-and-believers-religious-debate-in-the-western-intellectual-tradition. html

Robinson, B.A. (2014). Comparing Two Creation Stories: One from Genesis and the other from Babylonian Pagan Sources. Religious Tolerance. Retrieved from http:// www.religioustolerance.org/com_geba.htm

Robinson, B.A. (2011). Comparing & Contrasting the Two Creation Stories in Genesis. Religious Tolerance. Retrieved from http://www.religioustolerance.org/ ev_bibl.htm

Rose, Kenneth. (2000). King George V. London, England. Phoenix Press.

Sanders, E.P. (1993). The Historical Figure of Jesus. London, England. Penguin Books Ltd.

Sarfati, Jonathan. Archbishop's Achievement. Creation Ministries International. Retrieved from http:// creation.com/archbishops-achievement

Schirrmacher, Thomas. (2014). Inside the Vatican Synod on Family. Christian Post. Retrieved from http://www. christianpost.com/news/inside-the-vatican-synod-on-

family-pope-francis-delivers-bible-reading-on-love-
day-2-146887/

Scott, Gillan. (2012). The Queen–60 years of Defending
the Faith. God & Politics in the UK. Retrieved from
https://godandpoliticsuk.org/2012/02/06/the-queen-
60-years-of-defending-the-faith/

Scott, Gillan. (2015). Defender of the Faith: Queen
Elizabeth's Record Reign. Premier Christianity.
Retrieved from https://www.premierchristianity.com/
Blog/Defender-of-the-faith-Queen-Elizabeth-s-record-
reign

Scott, Ronald McNair. (1996). Robert the Bruce, King of
Scotts. New York, NY. Carroll & Graf.

Sheren, Marysa E. (2011). The Ethics of Disbelief. What
Does New Atheism Mean for America? An honors
thesis for the Department of Religion. Tufts University.

Sherwin, Frank. Human Evolution, An Update. Institute of
Creation Research. Retrieved from http://www.icr.org/
article/human-evolution-update/

Simpson, Jeffrey. (2016). Why the West is an outlier in Saudi-
Iranian rivalry. Toronto, Canada. Globe and Mail.

Skousen, W. Cleon. (1981). The 5,000 Year Leap: A Miracle
That Changed the World. Malta, ID. National Center
for Constitutional Studies.

Smenknhkare. Britannica Encyclopedia. Retrieved from
https://www.britannica.com/biography/Smenkhkare

Smith, Huston. (1991). The World's Religions. New York, NY.
Harper Collins Publishers.

Smith, Sally Bedell. (2012). Elizabeth The Queen, The Life of a Modern Monarch. New York, NY. Random House.

Smithsonian. (2015). Timelines of History. London, England. DK Penguin Random House.

Sproul, R.C. (2012). Are We Together? Sanford, FL. Reformation Trust Publishing, a division of Ligonier Ministries.

Stephen, Leslie and Pollock, Frederick. (1886). William K. Clifford Lectures and Essays. London, UK. Macmillan & Co.

The Annals of the Four Masters. Catholic Encyclopedia. Retrieved from http://www.catholic.org/encyclopedia/view.php?id=4812

The Annals of the Four Masters. Library Ireland. Retrieved from http://www.libraryireland.com/Pedigrees1/annals-four-masters.php

The Baptist Faith and Message. (2015). Southern Baptist Convention. LifeWay Press.

The Basics of Christian History. (2009). BBC. Retrieved from http://www.bbc.co.uk/religion/religions/christianity/history/history_1.shtml

The Lost Rivers of the Garden of Eden. (2016). KJV Bible. Retrieved from http://www.kjvbible.org/rivers_of_the_garden_of_eden.html

The Jacobite Heritage. (2003). Address to King James II at Kilkenny, March 22, 1689. Retrieved from http://www.jacobite.ca/documents/16890322.htm

The Printing Press. Lectures on Modern European Intellectual

History. The History Guide. Retrieved from http://www.historyguide.org/intellect/press.html

The Scottish Royal Dynasties 842 – 1625. The Royal Household. Retrieved from https://www.royal.uk/sites/default/files/media/stewart_family_tree.pdf

The Scythians. (2007). History World International. Retrieved from http://history-world.org/scythians.htm

The Scythian Family. Library Ireland. Retrieved from http://abcnews.go.com/Technology/evidence-suggests-biblical-great-flood-noahs-time-happened/story?id=17884533

The Sixteen Grandsons of Noah. Creation Ministries International. Retrieved from http://creation.com/the-sixteen-grandsons-of-noah

The Three Families of Man. Ray Stedman. Retrieved from https://www.raystedman.org/old-testament/genesis/the-three-families-of-man

Thiele, Edwin R. (1994). The Mysterious Numbers of the Hebrew Kings. Grand Rapids, MI. Kregel Publications.

Toth, Judy. (1996). Platform talk by Judy Toth. Ethical Society of St. Louis. Retrieved from http://www.ethicalstl.org/platforms/platform090096.php

Ussher, James. (2007). The Annals of the World. Green Forest, AZ. Master Books.

Vidmar, John, OP. (2005). The Catholic Church Through the Ages, A History. Mahwah, NJ. Paulist Press.

Walton, John H. (2015). The Lost World of Adam and Eve. Downers Grove, IL. InterVarsity Press.

Wiener, James. (2013). Scota: Mother of the Scottish People. Ancient History Encyclopedia. Retrieved from http://etc.ancient.eu/uncategorized/scota-mother-of-the-scottish-people/

Wofford, Taylor. (2014). Pope Francis's Remarks on Evolution Are Not That Controversial Among Roman Catholics. Newsweek. Retrieved from http://www.newsweek.com/pope-franciss-remarks-evolution-are-not-controversial-among-roman-catholics-281115

World Council of Churches. (2016). What is the World Council of Churches? Retrieved from http://www.oikoumene.org/en/about-us/

Witherspoon, Joseph Bailey. (1973). The History and Genealogy of the Witherspoon Family (1400–1972). Fort Worth, TX. Miran Publishers.

World Evangelical Alliance. (2016). Who We Are. Retrieved from http://www.worldea.org/whoweare/introduction

Zondervan NIV Study Bible. (2002). Grand Rapids, MI. Zondervan Corporation.

CPSIA information can be obtained
at www.ICGtesting.com
Printed in the USA
FSOW01n1842131017